THE COMPLETE GUIDE TO THE PARISH CHURCHES OF RUTLAND

THE COMPLETE GUIDE TO THE PARISH CHURCHES OF RUTLAND

ANDREW SWIFT

First published 2014 by Velox Books
208 Milligan Road, Aylestone. Leicester LE2 8FD

Copyright © Andrew Swift 2014

Text, design, photographs and illustrations © Andrew Swift 2014

All rights reserved. No part of this book may be reproduced or utilized in any form or by any means, electronic or mechanical, including photocopying, recording or by information storage or retrieval systems, without permission in writing from Velox Books.

Photographs: Cover, Braunston in Rutland All Saints
Frontispiece, Seaton All Hallows
This page, Tixover St Luke

ISBN 978-0-9575701-2-2

Printed and bound in Great Britain by Digital Wordcrafts and Tudor Bookbinding Ltd, Leicester

FOREWORD BY THE BISHOP OF PETERBOROUGH

I came to Peterborough Diocese from the north west just four years ago. Peterborough, Northamptonshire and Rutland (which together make up the Diocese) were new places for me. Very quickly I found my way around and learned to love this part of the country and its people.

Rutland is amazing whichever way you look at it. Our smallest county, with a population smaller than many towns (and smaller than some Church of England parishes), but a place of rich history, varied communities, great people, and over 50 stunning church buildings.

Rutland's church buildings are mainly medieval and mainly in very good condition. They are loved by their village communities, including those people who don't worship regularly. Maintaining medieval buildings is neither easy nor cheap, but much love and hard work goes into them, and my realistic hope is that the great majority of Rutland's church buildings are safe from any threat of closure for the foreseeable future.

I want to pay tribute to the clergy and churchwardens who work so hard, and to the teams of volunteers they lead, who ensure that these buildings are well cared for. They do this not just for love of the buildings, but as part of their worship of God and their determination to make God's love known in their communities. The church buildings, full of history though they may be, are not museums. They are places of prayer, worship and witness: places where Jesus Christ makes himself known as Lord and Saviour for all.

This book is another labour of love. I will come back to it regularly. It is thorough, careful and accurate. It is more than an essential work of reference for Rutland. It will I hope bring more people into these wonderful buildings where they can encounter the true church, the people who worship together - and where they can meet the living God.

The Right Reverend Donald Allister, Bishop of Peterborough   February 2014

INTRODUCTION

Following hot on the heels of my 'Parish Churches of Leicestershire' in two volumes, the appearance of a companion volume for Rutland should surprise no-one. The two counties have long historical and geographical links, and are usually (by folk from elsewhere) referred to in the same breath. Naturally, for the natives of the two counties, this lumping together is not viewed with much enthusiasm, because the fact is that Leicestershire and Rutland differ in many ways, and each population are well aware of those differences. Much can be explained by the big difference in size between the two counties, there simply isn't much room in Rutland for a great variety of landscapes, after all, it is the smallest county in the country (a status gloriously regained in 1997 after several 'dark years' of being subsumed in Leicestershire). And what magnificent landscapes this tiny area can boast! Many would have the county as the prettiest, acre for acre, in England. The rolling hills and gentle, green valleys, with charming small villages tucked away in the folds of the land, create an image that for many people is the essence of England. Simply put, it feels grand to be here, to walk in peace and tranquility and reconnect with a largely unsullied world, whether one is a birdwatcher, geologist, botanist, or walker, or just someone who appreciates a lovely view. The exploration and celebration of Rutland's churches has proved, for me, to be an unmitigated joy. They share all the attractions of the lovely villages and small towns that cradle them, and have a mellow beauty that is almost sentient. Over hundreds of years they have acquired a patina of rural grace that accurately reflects their settings. Much of that is due to the fact that Rutland was bypassed by the industrial revolution, its small settlements were never stained by 'dark, satanic mills', and even the large-scale quarrying of the honey-coloured and much sought after Jurassic Lincolnshire Limestone merely served to create even more nature reserves in the course of time. The one exception might be the vast working Ketton Quarry, but as any regular visitor to the quarry, myself included, will tell you, the older worked-out areas are already reverting readily back to nature and have thriving ecosystems, with rarities not found elsewhere in Rutland. So, this is a county that cries out to be explored and savoured, and its churches are amongst its greatest treasures. A great boon for the ecclesiastical enthusiast is that each church can be reached easily and there is no great distance between any of them. What's more, there are only 50 to visit! For one who has driven to every far flung corner of Leicestershire in the pursuit of its 316 (or so) active Anglican churches, this is not an insignificant attribute.

I have approached this book in a somewhat different way than its predecessor. In Leicestershire, it was necessary to introduce some minor restrictions on entries in order to render the project manageable. Thus that book covered only those Anglican establishments that were active, i.e. they were on the Church of England's list of working churches and retained regular services. Redundant and deconsecrated churches were left out, as were a very few churches that were outside Leicestershire's boundaries, despite being in the Diocese of Leicester. But here in Rutland, with only 50 Anglican churches, no such restrictions need be applied, so the redundant churches, such as Normanton, Wardley, Ayston and Burley on the Hill, are included. It is sad of course to see an 800 year old church close for regular services, but Rutland is lucky, as all its redundant churches have been taken on by conservation concerns and are kept in good order. A constant complaint about the churches in Leicestershire is that something like 70% are kept locked when not in use for services or other church activities. I explored the open or closed debate in the first volume of the Leicestershire book, and won't repeat it here. It is enough to say, I think, that in Rutland there is a wholly laudable policy of 'keep it open'. Nearly all of the 50 churches are open every day for allcomers, and even in the few cases where a church is kept locked, it is a relatively simple matter to obtain the key from a keyholder. Only on a couple of occasions was I slightly exercised in obtaining a key, but even then once I had located the right person, arrangements were amenably made. So three cheers for the church in Rutland!

As for the churches themselves, many are unexpectedly grand and there is a considerable range of ages and styles from Saxon to Victorian with fine examples of the best of those periods. Saxon remains are very rare and are represented mainly by a few carved stones (e.g. Greetham), but Market Overton has a complete tower doorway. Norman work is much more readily found and several churches retain round-arched arcades with typical carving (e.g. Morcott, which has several other good Norman features), Tixover has an excellent Norman tower and Tickencote, despite a cavalier C18th makeover which included many quasi-Norman features, has much of interest in the chancel. Essendine has a sadly much eroded Norman south doorway and Egleton a mysterious and intriguing tympanum. Many Rutland doorways have round heads with carved jambs and capitals, e.g. Hambleton, Wardley and Edith Weston. Stoke Dry has superb and vivaciously carved shafts associated with the chancel arch. Transitional and Early English fabric reflects a fascinating mixture of innovation and inertia through the late C12th into the C13th and there is much intermingling of styles, best represented in arcade detail. Sometimes certain new ideas were rapidly adopted and in others cases the old ideas held on. Thus, some churches have round-arched arcades with later types of pier morphologies and leaf carving in the capitals, while elsewhere the pointed arch is found with older styles of carved ornament on the piers. Visit Stretton, Ryhall and Essendine, for example, to see what this means. Some of this may be the result of later remodelling, of course. Peak time for Rutland's churches was the late C13th into the early C14th. From these Decorated times come the beautiful tracery in churches like Langham, Market Overton and Oakham and the tremendous steeples of Ketton and Empingham; also, the lovely arcades at Whissendine. However, it must be remembered that almost every church had its window tracery renewed by the Victorians, although they often repeated the original designs. Several churches received remodelling in Perpendicular times, and this again is best seen in the window tracery, e.g. Barrowden, Ryhall and Cottesmore (chancel). Later church works form only a minor part of Rutland's ecclesiastical story, but Brooke with its extensive C16th Elizabethan furnishing scheme must be seen, and Teigh also for its startling C18th collegiate interior. Tickencote is altogether unique and largely the result of a sweeping remodelling in the late C18th in a quasi-Romanesque style, and demands attention. Manton church has a nice late C18th chancel with characteristic windows, juxtaposed with a fine late Perpendicular south transept. Pickworth was a new church in 1821, and, while exceedingly modest and austere, is well worth a detour to see. Normanton is a hybrid of building schemes of 1764, 1826 and 1911 and was once worthy of notice, but these days, partly drowned and truncated, it is an adjunct to the leisure industry and has little to recommend it. Which brings the narrative up to the Victorians. No county escaped the all-pervasive attentions of their highly-organised neo-Gothic architectural juggernaut, and almost all Rutland churches were overhauled to a greater or lesser degree. In one extreme case a whole church was replaced (Bisbrooke); while others retained only their medieval towers and a few elements of their interiors, e.g. Burley on the Hill, Lyndon and Thistleton. Exton saw extensive renovation after the spire was hit by lightning in 1849, but is best known for its monuments. Most of Rutland's churches fell into the medium - modest restoration bracket, and some of the work is very fine, e.g. Uppingham (chancel), Oakham and Ashwell. It remains to be seen what will be the legacy of church works of more recent times, but clearly something significant is taking place. The conditions that typified church interiors prior to, say 1970, are no longer acceptable to today's churchgoers and church users, especially the younger ones brought up in centrally heated and comfortable homes. The demand is out there and insistent, and it says, we want our churches to be warm, comfortable and welcoming. No more hard benches, freezing temperatures and lack of basic amenities like toilets. And the churches are having to respond, many have already transformed their interiors, and the rest are preparing to follow suit. Thus, the face of church interiors is being turned around again, just like it was in Victorian times.

This book couldn't have been brought to fruition without the help of others, and I am pleased to acknowledge the assistance that has been given to me. The Right Reverend Donald Allister, Bishop of Peterborough, honoured me with his Foreword, for which I give thanks. For access to Barrowden, Pilton, Tinwell and Stretton churches I am grateful to the churchwardens and keyholders, and for the opportunity to photograph the interior of the now redundant church at Ayston I am pleased to thank Canon Rachel Watts, Rector of Uppingham. But, above all, I owe a deep debt to my partner Dr Joanne E. Norris, who relieved me of the chore of driving and provided excellent company, as well as adding many helpful suggestions and contributions.

The introduction can only give a flavour of the delights of the churches of Rutland, read on for the full story!

ABOUT THE AUTHOR

Andrew Swift was born and educated in Leicestershire. In 1973 he was employed by the Geology Department of Nottingham University, to work in an area he had always loved. There he began his own line of research into aspects of palaeontology, specifically the world of microfossils. Many professional papers followed and ultimately he was awarded the degree of Master of Philosophy in 1994. In 1990 he moved to the Geology Department of Leicester University, where he continued and broadened his research. He authored prestigious works for the Palaeontographical Society and the Palaeontological Association. On leaving university service in 2005, interest in geology was maintained by the continuation of a long association with the Geology Section of the Leicester Literary and Philosophical Society, during which he served as Chairman for many years. He continues to lecture and lead field excursions, and is the Geology Section's current editor.

Interest in churches came about relatively late in life and developed from a fascination with their history, architecture and place in the evolution of British society. A comprehensive two volume work on the parish churches of Leicestershire was published in 2013. This book on Rutland churches forms a complementary volume to the earlier work.

Andrew Swift is an Honorary Visiting Fellow in the Leicester University Geology Department and runs a small business restoring photographs and documents.

RUTLAND AND THE LOCATION OF CHURCHES IN THE TEXT

All churches are located by a letter/number reference on this map and also by an Ordnance Survey grid reference.

THE CHURCHES

Cottesmore St Nicholas

ASHWELL ST MARY B2, SK 866 137

St Mary from the north

Lots of interest for the church lover here in Ashwell church. The layout is standard, with west tower rebuilt with pyramid roof in the C19th, aisled nave, chancel, north and south chapels and south porch; however, the evolution of the building is interesting. At first sight the rather dour outline looks like a purely Victorian confection, with its odd stripy stonework on the tower and chancel, and overblown reticulated Gothic windows, but its roots are much older. Despite most if not all the windows being renewed in the C19th, the ballflower surrounds and Decorated tracery probably follow C14th century predecessors. Inside there are indications of even earlier foundation, as one arch in the north arcade is round and is supported by a contemporary C12th pillar. Other aspects of the interior, such as the remaining parts of the two arcades and the chancel and tower arches are also C13th or C14th. Yet the overwhelming impression inside is of a Victorian church, the result of a comprehensive restoration in 1851 by William Butterfield, his only major work in the county. Not only that, but this particular renovation was guided by the principles of the Gothic Revival movement, leaving a characteristic interior that was little altered in subsequent years. Much exterior fabric was also reworked or added by Butterfield (including the lych gate) but it is inside where his influence can most clearly be seen. All major and most minor fittings such as font, pulpit, chancel furniture, lovely reredos and the seating were replaced, yet in keeping with the beliefs of the ecclesiologists many medieval items deemed worthy of retention were kept and these, together with the excellent Victorian details, make for a compelling interior. Make sure the lights are on for an inspection, this is one of the more sepulchral churches in Rutland due to the wealth of stained glass and lack of a clerestory. The two chapels contain the best of the medieval survivals. There is a very rare early C14th wooden effigy of a knight, a tomb surmounted by the alabaster effigy of a priest and a much-graffiti'd incised slab, both late C15th. In the sanctuary is a recess for an Easter sepulchre, with niches. A fine Decorated period double sedilia is hidden by the organ.

St Mary from the east

Distinctive lych gate

Old clock mechanism

Looking east and west along the church

Font and tower arch

Incised slab

The tomb of a C14th priest

The C14th wooden knight

C19th sedilia and double piscina in the chancel

11

AYSTON ST MARY

B4, SK 859 010

St Mary and its rich covering of lichen

St Mary finally came to the end of its 900-odd year history as a working church in July 2012, when the final blow fell and the church was declared redundant by the Diocese of Peterborough. This was in response to a petition from the tiny Ayston congregation, who could no longer shoulder the financial burden of further repairs or even sustain basic maintenance. A terribly sad tale, but a very familiar one in these troubled times for the established church. The last service, which ironically attracted a full house, was held on July 29th 2012, and now silence hangs over the site. However, St Mary's future is thankfully secure, the Churches Conservation Trust is in the throes of acquiring the building, which is marvellous news for this fine edifice. The layout is a familiar one, with west tower, aisled nave, comparatively large chancel and south porch. C12th work can be seen in the north west angle of the nave, then a little later came the north aisle with its round-arched arcade. The south aisle is a Perpendicular replacement, but the south arcade, which has pointed arches and is of the late C13th or early C14th, remains from an earlier configuration. The tower and clerestory are probably late C14th in date, and the chancel may have been rebuilt in the C15th. The south porch may also be C15th. There have been no further additions to the fabric since that time, although it is clear that window tracery has been renewed in subsequent centuries. The Victorian hand was laid only lightly on St Mary, and therein lies most of its charm. Inside, box pews from around 1800 stand undisturbed from that time, and the plain, unpretentious little font is C18th. Most of the other furnishings are C19th or later, and the chancel was refitted in 1937. Two good C18th mural tablets can be found in the chancel and south aisle. The north arcade has two patches of scroll-like painting, and above the chancel arch a C17th royal arms peeps through in places. A very worn effigy in the shape of two figures is located in the north aisle, this is undoubtedly very old but many centuries outdoors has erased all detail. The east and south west windows of the south aisle have some excellent and unusually complete C15th and later stained glass.

Two views from the south

Looking east and west along the church   **?C14th effigy**

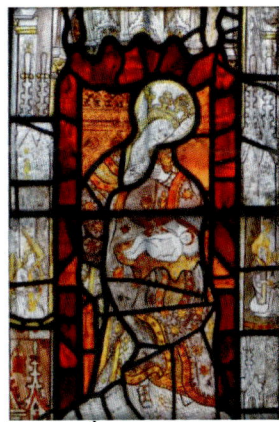

C17th roundel   **C15th stained glass**

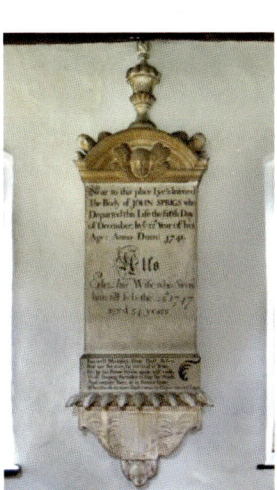

Part of a painted Arms   **The font**   **Piscina in chancel**   **Sprigs wall tablet**

13

BARROWDEN ST PETER
C4, SP 945 999

The splendid view from the south

This book would rapidly become very repetitious if all Rutland villages were to be described as 'picturesque', 'charming' or 'idyllic', so perhaps at this early stage it can be taken as read, and that Barrowden most definitely comes under those headings. St Peter is a major factor in that attractiveness and is a fine looking building, constructed of the local Lincolnshire Limestone. There is an admirable Perpendicular tower with long, stately belfry windows, topped by a classic broach spire. Much of the rest of the building, which consists of an aisled nave, chancel and south porch, shows C13th and C14th work with a nice mix of windows, e.g. the south window of the short south aisle has C13th plate tracery, and there are several typical Perpendicular examples. There is a good late C14th/early C15th clerestory. The south porch is an unusually early C13th example, with round headed doorway with several orders of mouldings in the arch; all four shafts are missing. The south doorway is also early and has a round arch and some very early ironwork. Inside, the two-bay south arcade is contemporary with its aisle and has a round pillar with stiff leaf carving on the capital, amongst which lurks a small carving of a human head. The north aisle, which was rebuilt in 1875, is similar, the capital of the single pillar and the responds lack embellishment. Both arcades have pointed arches, but the two arches of the arcade between the north chapel and the chancel are round, so possibly predate the nave arcades and be of similar date to the south porch. The interior lacks impact but contains some items worth seeking out. Opposite the south doorway on the north aisle wall is an imposing and very large wall tablet, intricately worked and bearing the date 1588. This is for Roland Durant. A tall, narrow wooden stand, which previously housed chained books, is an odd-looking piece and was reconstructed from salvaged sections of a pulpit broken up in 1875, at the time of a restoration. One of these sections bears the date 1605. The font is plain and octagonal and gives no clues to its date, but it is clearly old and may be C13th. There are medieval piscinas in both aisles and also in the chancel next to a double sedilia. On the chancel north wall near the altar is a brass inscription from a tomb of a rector who died in 1546.

From the south west and west

Looking east and west along the church — **The sanctuary**

The Durant tablet — **South aisle capital** — **Nave roof figure**

Piscina and sedilia in the chancel — **The font** — **Book stand/reading desk**

BELTON IN RUTLAND ST PETER   A4, SK 816 013

St Peter from Church Street

Ideally, the perfect village church should sit at the highest point surrounded by character cottages, with the village pub not too far away. Enter St Peter, which conforms to all of these requirements, and is a lovely building too, of ironstone and cream limestone. Like all churches, work of various ages makes up the fabric, but perhaps St Peter has a more complex history than most, made even more difficult to unravel by a postulated pre-C14th fire that took out an unknown portion of the building. The major survivor from before that alleged conflagration is the fine arcade to the south aisle (a north aisle was perhaps a victim of the fire and was never replaced); the arcade is C12th and is set very low on octagonal piers, with round arches of two chamfers. Not least of its attractions is the red, iron-rich sandstone used in its construction, and the inscrutable and mysterious heads and stiff leaf carving on certain capitals and the damaged east respond. A C13th lancet can still be found at the west end of the nave and some old fabric may survive low down in the chancel walls, but a major rebuilding in the C14th accounts for most of what remains today. The limestone ashlar tower probably originates from that time and was altered in the C15th. A Victorian refurnishing took place, as would be expected, but left a pleasantly intimate chancel and flamboyant organ case. There are several good features and fittings to beguile the visitor, beginning with the Early English font that is the first item encountered on entering. This has been through the wars, losing its supporting pillars at some stage, but the arches with dog-tooth are still attractive. Nearby is a vast wall memorial of 1762 with broken pediment and lots of gushing words about Rowland Roberts and his wife. More mural tablets adorn the walls, several of them worthy pieces from the C18th, but most are fading away beneath a layer of grime and are difficult to read these days. Easily missed is an incised slab of 1559, set into the floor immediately north of the chancel altar, this too is showing its age and seems to have been on a through route for much of its later history and part has worn away. The Victorian stained glass of 1898 in the chancel windows is of super quality and mostly depicts saints, all in pin-sharp detail and sparkling colours.

The church seen from the north — **Porch gargoyle** — **C14th/C15th tower**

Views along the church towards east and west — **Arcade details**

The sanctuary — **C13th font** — **Early C17th wall tablet**

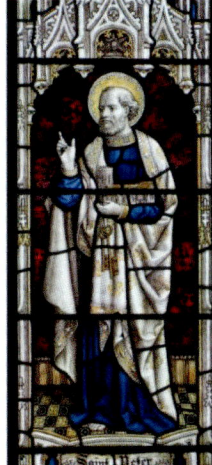

Roberts tablet, 1762 — **Section of incised slab, 1559** — **Excellent late C19th stained glass**

BISBROOKE ST JOHN THE BAPTIST   B4, SP 887 996

A brief gleam picks out St John

All is not what it seems at Bisbrooke. A visitor unversed in the history of St John the Baptist might, after due assessment, conclude that this is a C13th/C14th medieval building. So convincingly has the mellow ironstone fabric weathered and so authentic is the design that few would suspect that the building was constructed in 1871 and is only 143 years old. There was a medieval church on the site, but its dilapidated condition led to the complete rebuilding we see today. And the surprises don't end there, for those expecting a Victorian Gothic Revival interior with lots of stained glass, heavy furnishings and devotional gloom, the reality will come as a shock. Inside, the church is bright, airy and minimally, even starkly, furnished with the basics needed for running a church facility. There is an attractive floor of limestone flags, modern wooden chairs (but of a traditional design), simple pulpit, and unadorned chancel and sanctuary. After a while the realisation dawns that the church has no *clutter*. There are very few features or fittings either, so the sensation is decidedly odd for church lovers accustomed to finding their way around a church interior through the accumulated detritus of the ages. And it is really quite refreshing. All of that is down to a major refurbishment programme that ended in 2009, a refit that included underfloor heating, modern eco-sensitive kitchen and toilet facilities, and a complete freshen up. The down side is that there is very little here for the church historian to get their teeth into. The few features remaining are soon found and assessed, possibly the most interesting is a late C19th organ with a nicely carved panel at the top. An old parish chest somehow made it into the new interior, and the font is an unremarkable late Victorian example; the poor box/donations box may be of similar age. One touching feature is the 1st World War tablet which is flanked by two battlefield crosses. These were erected in haste in the fighting areas and were never intended to be permanent. Once upon a time, many parish churches housed examples brought back from overseas by grieving relatives, but these days they are getting quite rare. Whatever the arguments might be about such churches as St John, the fact remains that they represent a real attempt to update the Anglican church and create spaces that are attractive to modern congregations and also the community at large.

St John from the north east

… and from the east

North tower doorway

Looking along the church from the west and east

The simple sanctuary

The font

Old parish chest

1st World War battlefield crosses and memorial

Organ detail

19

BRAUNSTON IN RUTLAND ALL SAINTS   A3, SK 833 066

All Saints from the verdant churchyard to the south

All Saints is another star in the panoply of Rutland churches, appealing outside and with interest inside too. The plan is west tower with small spire, aisled nave, chancel with C19th vestry and south porch. A standard Perpendicular clerestory extends above the nave. The fabric is a patchy mixture of ironstone and Lincolnshire Limestone, reflecting the fact that different stone was preferred for each building or repair programme. The short tower was rebuilt in the early 1700's and looks as if it is missing a top stage, a feeling accentuated by the odd clock, which protrudes above the parapet as if it has lost its anchorage. Hidden away next to an external tower wall is a curious carved stone, one of the group known as sheela-na-gigs, which were perhaps fertility symbols or maybe just something to frighten away evil spirits. Certainly the grotesque face has all the qualities required for the latter. Its age could be anything between the C11th and C15th, but a date towards the earlier century looks most likely. Apart from a single C13th lancet window in the chancel north wall, little externally gives indications of a date of building prior to the C14th, but as soon as the south doorway is reached, it is clear that the church's origins are much further back in time. This is a fine Norman structure with an ornament of small nailheads in the outermost arch moulding and volutes on the shaft capitals. Inside there are other early indicators, particularly the chancel arch responds which have square abaci and scallop carving. The treasures inside are not immediately obvious, the interior is unexceptional, but a glance at the south and east walls of the south aisle reveals the first of them. These are two areas of probably C15th wall painting, depicting an obscure group of figures and images, but the instruments of the Passion and an angel are clear on the east wall and the outline of an altar on the south wall. There are some nice old brasses in the south aisle, one shows a man and wife, with dedicatory plate (c.1596) and the other a coat of arms with a dedicatory plate (c.1642). The big, square font is a battered C12th example, with shafts at the angles. The war memorial and other windows are by Kempe & Co, incorporating their wheatsheaf symbol overlain with a tower, the logo from 1907. The churchyard is pleasantly undulating and attractive.

From the north east   **….. and the north west**   **Sheela-na-gig**

South doorway   **Views east and west along the nave**

One of the areas of wall painting   **Cheseldyn brass of 1596**   **The font**

Examples of the Kempe glass, plus logo   **Selection of wall tablets**   **Stone coffin**

21

BROOKE ST PETER

B3, SK 850 057

The best time to see St Peter is in the Spring

Now here's a quintessential picture of rural England's heartland, rolling hills, verdant countryside and the perfect little hamlet, with, of course, the perfect country church. Many people, if asked to draw up their idealised 'dream village', might well come up with somewhere like Brooke. No pub though, which is a shame. St Peter sends church lovers into rapture, its atmosphere redolent of the past and vividly stimulating, no wonder film makers seek it out too. But there's more to it than pure aesthetics, this is a most intriguing church, because substantial parts of it date from the reign of Elizabeth 1st, a time of little church building or modification. The interior fittings remain intact from that time, benches and box pews, stalls, screens, altar rails – there is characteristic Elizabethan woodwork everywhere. It is simple, tasteful and considered, with careful use of space to avoid cluttering, so often a fault of the Victorians. Of course the latter had to have their input during the C19th, but beyond a little rearranging of the fittings they appear to have done very little. Elizabethan interiors like Brooke are rarely seen and that is what makes the effect of St Peter so vivid. Yet this is not wholly an Elizabethan building, it is soon apparent that its origins are much deeper in time, a fact brought home immediately by the south doorway with its characteristic Norman carving in the arch. Inside, the Norman element is further reinforced by the handsome round-arched arcade and a roughly contemporary font, which stands nearby. The former has typical carving on the capitals and the latter is a substantial, square item with arcade carving and solid stone base. The tower and its fine arch to the nave are C13th, but the nave itself is almost impossible to date, older than the rest of the church except the tower but now with Tudor windows. The east end of the aisle was developed as a chapel and is still screened off with balustered panelling; it contains the impressive tomb of Charles Noel who died in 1619. The Noels later decamped to Exton, and their memorials are what make Exton church such a mecca for church lovers. Set in to the floor of the chapel are several interesting old grave covers. There is lots more, on no account should Brooke and its unique interior be missed.

Two views from the west

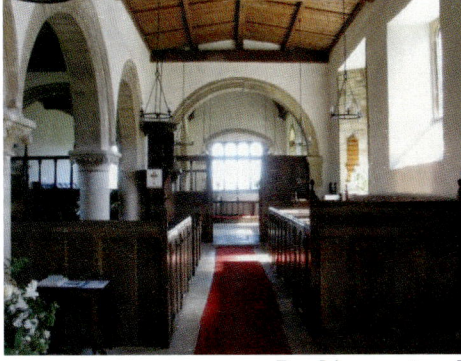

The Norman doorway **Looking east and west along the church**

Elizabethan woodwork in the chancel

Pulpit and other woodwork **The font** **Charles Noel's tomb**

BURLEY HOLY CROSS   B2, SK 883 102

Holy Cross from the south

Burley on the Hill has a long and noble history, with the highest area long being reserved for lordly houses and estates. Several magnificent residences have stood on the site. The village of Burley itself was previously much larger than the present hamlet and probably extended up the hill before the 'quality' moved in. It was in those days that a church was first built on the site, to serve the village. Evidence in the present church suggests that may have been in the C12th. Later, as the influence of the lords of the manor increased, they largely claimed the church for themselves, effectively turning it into an estate church, which it has been at least since the C17th. With the decline of the manor in the C20th, the eventual conversion of the big house into very posh dwelling 'units', and the tiny size of Burley village, it was no real surprise when the church was declared redundant in 1984. Since then it has been in the care of the Churches Conservation Trust. The present Holy Cross church has an overarching Victorian stamp, courtesy of a sweeping programme of rebuilding and refitting by Pearson in 1869-70. Externally, the C14th tower is the only substantial part remaining from the medieval church, and that was restored in 1913. The rest of the church consists of aisled nave, chancel with aisles under one sweeping roof, and north porch. The north porch houses the main doorway, facing the village. For the convenience of the people of the Hall, a corridor runs from the big house into the chancel. Whilst the exterior retains little evidence of antiquity, Pearson did at least leave some significant medieval elements intact inside. Chief of these are the two arcades, the north is C12th and has round arches, and the south is C13th with pointed arches. The tower arch, though restored, is contemporary with the tower. The stylish font is C15th and has varied tracery in its panels. By the tower arch lie the effigies of a knight and his lady, from the 1400's. At some point, probably during a move, the poor knight lost his lower body. There are two fine memorials to members of the Finch family, who owned the manor in the C18th and 19th centuries, the best being a very sentimental statue commemorating Lady Charlotte Finch, who died in 1813.

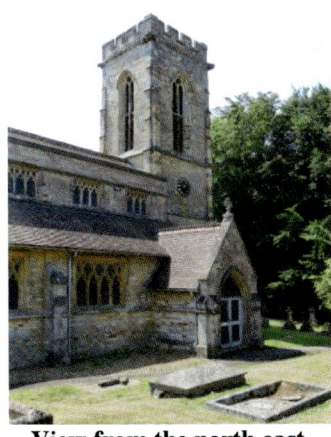
View from the north east

Finch graves

The sanctuary

Looking along the nave to the chancel

Norman north arcade

Finch memorials (interior)

Wall tablet, 1791

Late C15th knight and lady

The pulpit

The font

Victorian coronae lucis

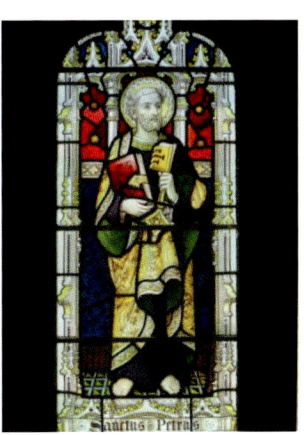
Saint Peter

25

CALDECOTT ST JOHN THE EVANGELIST B5, SP 868 937

St John from the south

Caldecott is the most southerly of Rutland villages, and lies very close to the Leicestershire and Northamptonshire borders. The church of St John is an attractive building, drawing the eye on account of its pale limestone spire. This has had a chequered career, and had to be rebuilt at least twice. Two dates are recorded on its stonework, 1638 and 1797. A reminder of the 1797 incident, when the spire was struck by lightning, stands by the porch entrance. This is the topmost portion of the spire which fell in that year. Recent reports suggest that the spire is once again giving problems, and needs repair. The church consists of tower and spire, nave with a south aisle, chancel, south porch and organ chamber of 1908. A north aisle was projected, but was never built. An arch in the west wall of the organ chamber, through which the aisle would have been accessed, remains. The original C12th building consisted of a short nave with even shorter square-ended chancel. A small round-headed window with wide internal splay from that original church survives in the chancel south wall. That first building was extended both east and west in the late C13th, the south aisle built and the chancel arch added. A length of original wall remains in the arcade at the west end, before the final archway. Tower and spire followed in the C14th. The porch bears the date 1648. Thorough Victorian restorations left a heavy footprint inside, and little has changed since that time, except for the removal of pews in the south aisle and further minor modifications in 1982. A curious C13th square font sits near the south entrance, its corners crudely chamfered to accommodate some equally crude geometrical carving. On the sides are carvings of arches, again very rustic work. Another surviving old feature is the rood loft opening to the south of the chancel arch, this retains some original steps. The only mural tablet of any age is in the vestry/organ chamber, this dates from 1712; nearby is a C18th chest. Typical Victorian features include 'improving texts' on mural banners and the chancel arch, and a large Victorian royal arms which resides above the chancel arch. In the churchyard an impressive collection of table tombs are gathered immediately west of the tower.

From the north west and west   Tombs near the tower

Looking east and west along the church

Victorian mural banner   Rood loft opening   Sedilia and piscina

The font   Mural tablet of 1712   Victorian Royal Arms

CLIPSHAM ST MARY

D1, SK 970 164

From the south

Clipsham has a reputation and fame far beyond its modest borders, the reason for which can be seen in the walls of St Mary. These are built with the famous Clipsham Stone, a local variant of the Lincolnshire Limestone, especially prized as a building stone. It is still worked a few miles from the village and has been used in some of Britain's most prestigious buildings. It has an attractive creamy yellow hue and imbues buildings constructed of it with a most beguiling appearance. St Mary is no exception. The church is best known for its unusual and unique spire, somewhat dumpy in appearance but bursting with architectural imagination. It and the tower into which it blends so effectively in the broach style, are $C13^{th}$, as is much of the rest of the fabric. The plan of St Mary apart from the tower/spire is aisled nave, chancel with north aisle and south porch. The nave aisles extend onto the tower and enclose its basal portion. The chancel aisle was developed as a chapel, but now sees service as a vestry and organ chamber. Both arcades have round arches but only the northern one is Norman, the south arcade is Early English. Only one arch, the westernmost one in the north arcade, is ornamented, with odd chevron/zig-zag carving enriched with leaf and ball ornament. In the north aisle abaci are square and the capitals carved with lobes. The chancel arcade to the aisle/chapel has pointed arches. Victorian woodwork dominates the interior and medieval elements are rare. Of the latter, the $C12^{th}$ font is worthy of note, being a deep tub with a rim of ornament. A small length of $C12^{th}$ string course with scallop ornament can be found in the south aisle. Dotted around, a few corbel heads have survived from the church's early years, their untutored carving contrasting with the slick Victorian angels in the chancel. The south aisle piscina with its internal ogee arch is probably $C14^{th}$. The reredos of c.1860 is expertly carved and detailed, and features the last supper, transfiguration and ascension. The pulpit is also intricately carved and sits on a substantial stone base. Of the wall tablets, the best is one of 1796 to the Rev'd Snow. A much deteriorated brass tablet in the chancel was designed by Pugin. A most peculiar painted Ten Commandments board resides on the nave north wall, featuring two biblical 'prophets'.

  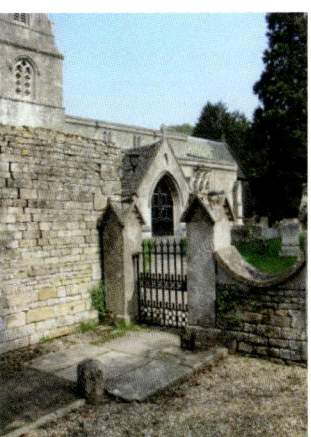 

From the south east   **The tower**   **The approach**   **The C12th font**

Looking from the west and east along the church

Arcades   **The pulpit**    **Corbels**

The Ten Commandments   **Snow wall tablet**   **Stained glass**

29

COTTESMORE ST NICHOLAS   C2, SK 902 136

From Main Street in Cottesmore

Cottesmore is the third largest settlement in Rutland, behind Oakham and Uppingham, its daily life enhanced for many years by nearby RAF Cottesmore and its personnel. The RAF operation was closed down in 2011 but continuity was ensured when the base was taken over by units of the army and renamed Kendrew Barracks. Cottesmore, even before the base was created, was a village of some importance and the parish church of St Nicholas is ample testimony to that. It is an assertive statement in the heart of the village, and possesses a handsome outline, made up of a particularly grand tower with broach spire, aisled nave, long chancel and a bold south porch, previously with an upper room. A small vestry attached to the north of the chancel has recently been extended to house a meeting room. Corbel tables of quirky heads and figures run along the nave, aisles and at the top of the tower. Building stone is almost exclusively Lincolnshire Limestone in ashlar form. The evolution of the building has taxed experts for many years, there is work of $C12^{th}$ to $C19^{th}$ but it seems the major building phases, as with so many churches, were during the $C13^{th}$ and $C14^{th}$. The oldest fabric consists of a resited, finely carved Norman south doorway, and pilaster buttress to the north of the tower. This probably marked the westerly limit of an original $C12^{th}$ building, whilst inside a short stretch of wall before the easternmost arch of the north arcade may mark its easterly extent. Much work in the $C13^{th}$ resulted in the tower and spire and an extension eastwards of the chancel. The presence of a former north chapel hereabouts is indicated by the survival of a tiny section of the arcade to it, with nailhead, which was exposed during Victorian restorations and left open to view. The interior is enhanced by the tall arcades, which lend a refined air, and the tastefully appointed chancel. The number of interesting fittings is a little disappointing for such a fine church, but the font alone almost makes up for that. The octagonal bowl is $C14^{th}$, and has two arcades on seven sides, the other one is blank. But it is the much older base that excites, on two of its sides are mystical and primitive carvings of the crucifixion and a bishop, possibly pre-$C12^{th}$. The pulpit is Jacobean and there are a few rather indifferent wall tablets.

 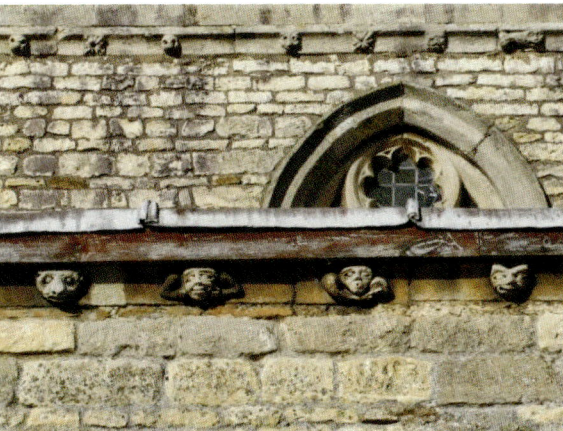 

South east view   **Corbel tables**   **Norman south doorway**

Looking east and west along the church

Remains of chapel arcade   **The font**   **Font figure 1**

Font figure 2   **Piscina**   **Lead tablet**   **The pulpit**

31

EDITH WESTON ST MARY   C3, SK 927 054

St Mary from Church Lane

When the builders of St Mary began their work in the C12th, never in their wildest dreams could they have imagined that one day the waters of a vast lake would be lapping almost at the doors of Edith Weston's houses. Nor, for that matter, could any generation of villagers until the middle of the C20th. But now, Rutland Water is so much part of the landscape that it seems as if its always been there, and Edith Weston is almost a holiday resort in fine weather. The village and its church of St Mary were lucky, Nether Hambleton and most of Middle Hambleton were drowned and Normanton's church of St Matthew was half filled with concrete, the top half then preserved above the waters for the benefit of tourists and the wedding industry. Back to St Mary; this is a small church, but with an unusual and expansive plan, consisting of C14th tower and spire, modest nave with two narrow aisles and a much higher chancel with steeply-pitched roof. What is unusual is that the nave has a south transept and the chancel has two, the northern one for the organ and the southern one for a chapel. Add the south porch and the result is an irregular and curious layout. Inside, that plan creates the feeling of a warren, with arches and arcades between all the units, but a most fascinating one with something interesting around every corner. The church's C12th origins are immediately apparent in the north arcade, with its round arches. The south arcade is also round-arched, but post-1200. The chancel arch is the oldest part of the fabric, with square abaci, stiff-leaf and other carving characteristic of the mid-C12th. Amongst the intriguing array of carvings is a vertical strip between the major and minor chancel piers with primitive nailhead-type carving. East of the chancel arch, all is Victorian, thanks to a restoration in the mid 1860's, with powerful vaulted roofs, a fine reredos of 1896 and other exotic touches. Many excellent and substantial memorials adorn the church, chief amongst them being the massive Holford/Lucas tablet in the south transept and another ornate tablet c.1733 in the north aisle for Sir Gilbert Heathcote, by Rysbrack. A stone mensa forms an altar in the north aisle. The plain font is very old, but undateable. Crudely carved medieval bench ends have been incorporated into some of the furniture.

South transepts and graveyard

Mensa altar in the north aisle

Looking east and west along the church

The south chapel

North aisle

Detail around the chancel arch

Holford/Lucas memorial

Ancient poppyheads

1806 Royal Arms

The font

33

EGLETON ST EDMUND B3, SK 876 075

St Edmund's clean lines seen from the south

Egleton St Edmund is probably more visited and better known now than it has ever been, and that is due to the proximity of Rutland Water, and, more importantly, the cycle trails that wind around it. One of these goes past the south side of St Edmund and on fine days a large number of cycles use it, their riders frequently stopping off to view the church. That is good news for the old building and also its new visitors, because this is a church with a lot to offer. Little of the treasure trove within is hinted at by the rather boxy exterior, which consists of tower with spire, the base is medieval but the upper stage and spire are C18th, nave without aisles and fairly long chancel. Once there was a Decorated north aisle, which can clearly be confirmed by the continued existence of its arcade entombed within the north wall of the nave; outside, the contrasting colour of the infill of the arches is very apparent. There is a tunnel-like, windowless south porch which creates just the right atmosphere of mystery in which to best appreciate the remarkable south doorway, the first of Egleton's gems to greet the visitor. This is unmistakeably old and features some amazing Norman carving, especially in the tympanum, rich in arcane and enigmatic symbolism. On entering, St Edmund's misty origins are further confirmed by a strange, square font, which has geometrical and cross-like carvings. If anyone was still in any doubt, a glance towards the chancel arch will finally confirm that St Edmund did indeed begin life when the Normans ruled England. This has a grand round arch, but, again, it is the flamboyant carvings on the thin shafts to the side and on the imposts that make it special. Above the chancel arch is what looks initially like a patch of rotting plaster but which on examination proves to be a heavily degraded, painted George II royal arms. Other worthy objects include a somewhat reconstructed C15th screen, once no doubt across the chancel arch, but adapted for similar service for the tower arch. Also at the west end are a series of battered bench ends with crudely carved poppyheads. There is a large squint in the wall between nave and chancel. Some corbel heads are now marooned on the nave wall when the roof was remade. There are three C18th wall tablets and much more to see. St Edmund is one of Rutland's more intriguing churches.

The church from the south west **Norman south doorway** **Arch and tympanum**

The nave showing chancel arch and painted royal arms **Looking west along the nave**

Tower arch and screen **C12th font** **Stone heads and C15th poppyheads**

Chancel arch details **George II royal arms** **Tomson memorial of 1776**

EMPINGHAM ST PETER C3, SK 951 085

St Peter from Church Street

Here is a grand old church which enjoys a dominating position in Empingham. The C14th tower and spire combination are a powerful presence and look down imperiously on Church Street. The tower west doorway is magnificent, with orders of shafts and mouldings in two ornate surrounds, both topped with ogee arches. Appropriately, this doorway is the main entrance to St Peter, so all visitors have the best possible introduction to its enticing interior. The rest of St Peter (aisled nave, chancel, north and south transepts, south porch and north vestry) features much C13th work, some of it early like the south arcade with its retooled round arches, and some a little later like the transepts and chancel. North and south doorways are also C13th. Perpendicular changes saw the nave heightened for a clerestory and probably the formidable crenelation which adorns all but the chancel. A Victorian makeover of 1894-5, though not too drastic, left a strong C19th feel to the interior, mitigated by the provision of chairs instead of pews. There is a great deal to see inside, which belies the initial impression of emptiness created by the wide open spaces of the complex plan and high nave roof. The south arcade, already alluded to, is the oldest thing on view, but there is lots more C13th fabric and fittings to explore. The finest architecture seen in the fittings can be found in the chancel, in the form of the delicately carved and quite delightful double piscina and triple sedilia set. A number of probably C13th coffin lids can be found in the north transept, one housed in a recess. All are in poor condition. Of later medieval date are patches of wall painting which have been exposed; these are dotted around the walls, especially in the transepts. Most of the painting is of rather nondescript decorative type, but in one area figures can be made out and it has been suggested that a scene involving the Virgin Mary is depicted. Some fragments of C15th glass are reset into windows in the north transept, most are armorial or unidentifiable pieces, but some figurative work can be seen including one male face which is finely drawn and has a most enigmatic look. The font is an ornate, but stiff, piece of 1895. The plain pulpit is late C17th. A pretty limestone wall sets off the raised churchyard to perfection.

Views from the south east and north

Looking east and west along the church

Lovely double piscina and triple sedilia set  **Victorian font** **C15th roof angel**  **Medieval grave covers**

A face from the past 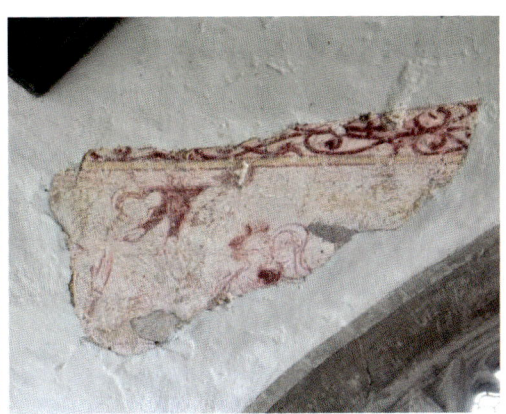 **Wall painting**  **Pre-1800 Hanoverian Royal arms**

ESSENDINE ST MARY

E2, TF 490 128

From the church gate

If driving through Essendine from the south west, St Mary is easily missed, as it is set back off the road and hidden from view until one has driven almost into Lincolnshire. However, coming the other way, the site is clearly seen. The church of St Mary is a modest structure consisting of nave and higher chancel and western bellcote. It has fabric dating back to the C12th, there was much restructuring in the C13th and more far-reaching rebuilding and refitting in the C19th. There is a C14th low-side window in the chancel south wall, with quatrefoil opening externally. Reaching the churchyard gate, an unexpected sight greets the visitor, for running left and right and encircling St Mary is what looks like a moat. It is indeed a moat, but how many churches can boast one of those? Further investigation on the north side of the church reveals another contiguous moat extending around a much bigger site. The keen mind may quickly work out that this is the likely site of a medieval moated manor or perhaps something even earlier like a castle. From there recourse to the literature is necessary, and this tells us that 'Essendine Castle' stood here, and St Mary is thought to be its chapel. Much still remains conjecture, but, whatever, the layout is fascinating and most unusual. More excitement is generated by the south doorway, an intricately carved Norman structure, parts of which may be even older. The carvings are now disappearing under the onslaught of the English weather, but may depict Adam and Eve and hunting scenes of a decidedly secular nature. More can be found on the east jamb of the internal doorway, these are in better condition, but equally mysterious. Both men and beasts seem to be involved and hunting again seems to be the theme. On the church's north side another doorway shows much simpler Norman geometrical carving in the lintel. Inside, more Norman work is exhibited in the chancel arch, once round-arched but now reconfigured to be pointed. The plain deep font may also be Norman. The chancel piscina is C13th. There the interest ends, there is little else to rouse the church enthusiast. The interior fittings are nearly all regulation Victorian. A few older mural tablets have survived from the C18th and are typical of their time. The modern glass in the east window is striking.

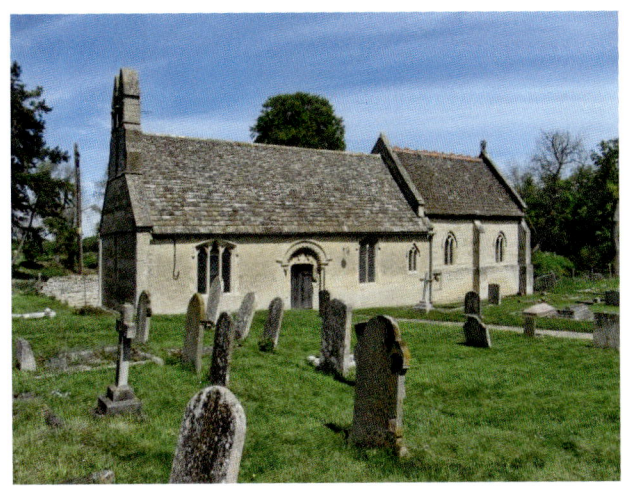

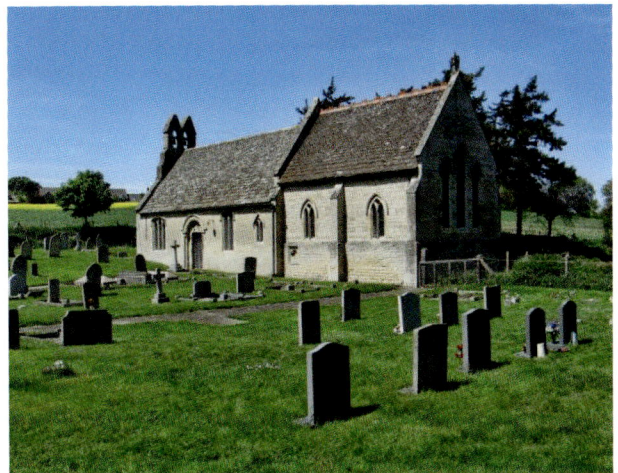

The church from the south west and south east

South doorway   **Looking east and west along the church**

Chancel arch  **Interior door jamb carving**  **East window**  **The mystery object**

Mural tablets  **Piscina**  **The font**

EXTON ST PETER & ST PAUL   C2, SK 921 112

St Peter amongst its host of gravestones

Nationally important churches are rare in the East Midlands, maybe there are only 10-20 in total, but Exton certainly qualifies as one of those. Yet it isn't the building itself that has generated the fame, fine though it is, its what's inside it. St Peter and St Paul contains one of the finest collections of baronial monuments and memorials anywhere in the UK, of fabulous quality and extravagance. All over the church they can be found, a wonderful feast for the eyes and senses. Two of Britain's best sculptors contributed pieces, Grinling Gibbons and Joseph Nollekins, and other monuments are of scarcely less importance. The presence here of such a collection is due to the connection with Exton Park, the seat of the Dukes of Gainsborough, the Noels and their relations. This was 'their' hall church, and they ensured that it became the repository of the family memorials. Back to the building for a moment, because this too can tell a fascinating story. Up until 1843, a C13th to C14th church stood here, and then nature intervened and lightning struck the tower, which crashed down into the nave and chancel. The church was soon rebuilt, a process begun by Carpenter in the mid 1840's and finished by Pearson in 1852-4. As much as possible the original plan was followed for the rebuild, especially with regard to the complex tower, which was faithfully reproduced. A little more liberty was taken with the rest of the building and it is hard to unravel what of the medieval structure was left and what was replaced. The medieval font survived, and is a busy C14th affair, richly carved with arches and heads. Two of the windows and arcade details including the stiff leaf carving may also be original. Noel funerary flags hang from the nave walls and much else about the church is admirable, but one always returns to the monuments. There are three important tombs, the oldest from the later C14th, and three massive and intricately ornate standing wall memorials, the biggest being the Gibbons piece for Viscount Campden and his considerable family. The tomb of Anne, Lady Kinlosse, of c.1628 is simply lovely. Many other 'lesser' monuments adorn the building, and a leisurely examination is recommended. They are kept in fine condition and the most important are highlighted for our pleasure.

The church from the south west   **Tower gargoyle**   **The font**

Looking east and west along the nave    **Harington tomb (c.1530)**

The grand memorials (the 'Kelway' monument c.1580, James & Lucy Harington c.1592, 3rd Viscount Campden c.1693)

l-r: Baptist Noel c.1771, Anne Lady Kinlosse (b-ground Bennett Noel c.1766), Anne Lady Kinlosse c.1627, James Noel c.1691

GLASTON ST ANDREW

St Andrew from the south east approach

In a county of very fine churches, St Andrew is not in the front rank, but is still a most appealing building. It can also boast one of the few central towers in Rutland, a genuine C12th version, though much revamped subsequently. The dumpy spire was added in the early C13th. All the rest of the church has been renewed on several occasions and received a thorough Victorian 'going-over', yet it retains an antique ambience. The many changes over the years are reasonably well-documented and these written records explain St Andrew's evolution. Apart from fabric in the tower, the oldest thing on view externally today is a short length of string course on the nave south wall which terminates in a worn head. The north aisle was rebuilt in the C14th and extended to enclose the base of the tower. A door was cut in the tower north wall to access the 'new' eastern part of the aisle. Most windows are replacements but feature an interesting range of tracery, especially the west window with its 'swirly' lights in the head. Inside, the pier and responds of the eastern section of the arcade are part of the original Norman church and feature waterleaf carving in varying styles on the capitals. Fairly unusually, ironstone was used for the arcade, with some local limestone appearing in the arches. The arches were originally round, but were replaced with pointed versions in the C14th. Like all such churches, the excellent chancel beyond the central tower is imbued with an enhanced sense of the mysterious, and in more liturgical days that must have helped with generating the required awe from the congregation, seated some distance away in the nave and peering through the void of the tower. Most fittings are not of great historical or archaeological interest, but there are some worth seeking out. In the chancel the partially renewed C14th sedilia and piscina, though plain, are dignified, and next to the altar is a C14th coffin lid with a foliated cross and an inscription running around the edges. Two old heads sit at the apices of the arcade arches. A couple of excellent C18th tablets can be found on the aisle north and west walls. Quality stained glass by Heaton, Butler & Bayne adorns several windows. The font is a staid, C14th style Victorian example. Parts of an old screen are incorporated into the pulpit and reading desk.

Three views of St Andrew, from the south west, east and west

The nave looking towards the central tower arch  **The chancel**

Capital carvings   **Nave roof** **Carvings in stone and wood**

The font  **Heaton, Butler & Bayne stained glass**  **Coffin cover and wall tablet**

GREAT CASTERTON ST PETER & ST PAUL   D2, TF 101 088

From across the old Great North Road

Great Casterton's church is often described as an unrestored medieval building. However, St Peter is not a wholly unrestored church, left just as it was in the C13th/14th. In fact there is a crisp, up-to-date feel inside, and much renewal, with modern seating, altar and reredos, plus a restored nave roof and a chancel that was restored in 1930. The vestry was built only in 1982. That said, the number of medieval features and survivals is certainly greater than in most churches, and these make an exploration of St Peter a rewarding experience. The church consists of a nave with short aisles, chancel, south porch and modern vestry. All that is largely C13th or C14th, built around and upon an C11th or C12th predecessor. At the west end, within the westernmost bay of the nave, is a C15th tower with outsize pinnacles and elaborate weathervane. Battlements bristle above every wall. Even before the church is entered, there are several points of interest externally. A statue sits in a niche above the east windows, and despite some debate, it probably represents one of the church's two dedicatees; nearby on the chancel south wall is an C18th tablet. Also on the south side, set into the aisle, is an interesting, probably C13th, coffin lid in a niche. This is of the type known as 'head and feet', where only the deceased's head and feet are sculpted, shown as if through two small windows. Inside, next to the tower north wall, is a better preserved example. The chancel has some good Early English lancet windows. The porch is also C13th, with an impressive outer doorway. Inside, the round-arched arcades sweep high, and there is a range of leaf carving on the capitals. Old piscinas, two each side, reside in the aisles. The Norman font is deep and square, with lozenge ornament. Patches of medieval floral wall painting are exposed, especially in the north aisle by the east window. The pulpit is a stately C18th example, with tester; the altar rails are also C18th. A well-preserved effigy of a C13th priest lies in a niche in the south aisle. Set into the top of the east tower arch is a tympanum bearing the arms of George II and a motto. The tower roof is vaulted, supported by armorial corbels.

St Peter from the south and north  **Porch doorway**

Looking east and west along the church

Wall tablet **South and north aisle piscinas**  **The font**  **The pulpit**

Geo. II arms, capital carving  **Wall painting, north aisle** **Priest and 'head and feet' effigies**

45

GREETHAM ST MARY C2, SK 925 147

St Mary and its splendid tower and spire

The highlight of St Mary is the very fine tower and broach spire combination, which soars above the village. In an area where broach spires are not unusual, this is one of the best. It has some similarities with the slightly less imposing spire at neighbouring Cottesmore, and its tempting to surmise that the same masons were involved, although there is no evidence for that. The rest of the church, which consists of aisled nave, chancel, south porch and C19th vestry, is somewhat overshadowed by the spire, but is still an attractive construction, finished in the local Lincolnshire Limestone stone. The church as seen today had its origins in the C13th, but fragments of C11th carving set into the south aisle west wall suggest an earlier structure existed on the site. The C12th font, which is shaped like a Norman capital, with ornament of large leaves ending in volutes at the corners with a band of strong dogtooth decoration above, may also have resided in the earlier church. The nave and chancel are probably early C13th, with the south aisle added a little later. The odd configuration seen at the west end of the chancel south wall externally was built to enable the widening of the chancel arch; peeping through the stonework here are traces of an arch which may have led to a south chapel. The porch has a fine outer doorway, with big shafts, several orders in the arch and hoodmould with heads. The clerestory was added quite early, in Decorated times, indicated by the small circular openings in the north wall, with quatrefoil windows. A corbel table with a variety of masks runs beneath the plain nave parapet. Internally, the first objects encountered are the oldest, these are the quite large Saxo-Norman fragments in the south aisle west wall, and the font. Above the high, graceful north arcade are the round windows of the clerestory. A George I royal arms is set above the blocked north doorway. Penetrating a little further into the interior a nice, though somewhat reconstituted, Jacobean pulpit is still doing sterling service. The altar rails are typical C18th examples. Best of all, the sanctuary is panelled around with rare and unusual woodwork depicting Old Testament themes, probably C17th.

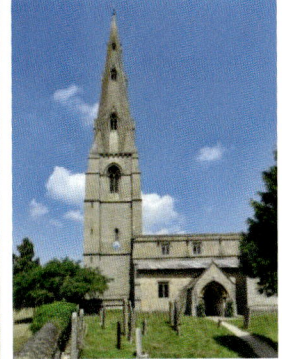

St Mary from the south west and south    **The chancel**

Looking west and east along the church

Jacobean? panelling in the sanctuary    **George I royal arms**    **The font**

Two fragments of C11th carving    **The pulpit**    **Fine glass**

47

HAMBLETON ST ANDREW   C3, SK 900 076

The view from the south

Hambleton changed in the late C20th from a sleepy little village to one of the hubs of Rutland Water, in fact it is as intimately associated with the lake as it is possible to be, sited as it is on a narrow promontory projecting out into it. This association has transformed Hambleton and there can scarcely be a day in the year when the village doesn't receive visitors, often in large numbers. So it is to everyone concerned's credit that Hambleton remains a lovely, relatively unspoiled spot, unpolluted by ice cream parlours, gift shops, tea rooms and the like. Just a pub and a hotel, which were always there. All that new attention has benefited St Andrew, which now receives more visitors than it could ever have dreamed of, and the old church seems a lot cheerier because of it. In fact, St Andrew is a very fine church with much to offer, so all sides have benefited. Its roots are old, at least extending back into Norman times, when the venerable and ornate south doorway was constructed. Most of the rest of the church, which consists of west tower with short spire, aisled nave, chancel, south porch, vestry running off the north of the tower and organ chamber, is of the C13th and C14th. Some features and fittings from those times are still with us today, like the arcades, tower arch, plain chamfered font and two 'head and feet' effigies, one near the tower missing its bottom half. Yet, unusually, it is the C19th aspects of St Andrew that give it its greatest appeal. In the late 1890's a wealthy philanthropist, Walter Marshall, moved to Hambleton to be near the hunts he supported. He was soon engaged in good works for the neighbourhood, and made the church one of his main priorities. In conjunction with the architect J. Lee he rebuilt the chancel and refitted it and the rest of the church with a suite of high quality, arts and crafts inspired furnishings. Since those days, the congregation of St Andrew has jealously conserved all of this work, and to their great credit, we can witness today a full Victorian liturgical vision, unchanged from the late C19th. Highlights are the marvellous chancel stained glass and reredos by James Egan, the altar frontals, other tapestry work in the Lady Chapel by Alfred Hemmings, lovely lectern, pulpit and other fine woodwork. And don't miss the organ case angels!

St Andrew from the south east 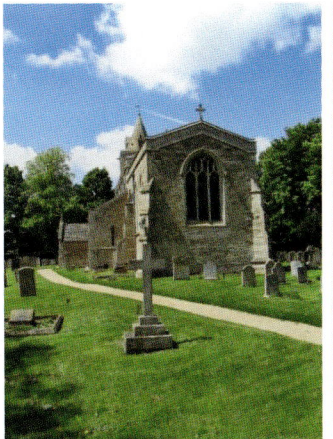 | From the east  | Norman south doorway

Looking east and west along the church

Classic late Victorian chancel  | 'Head and feet' effigy  | The amazing organ case carving

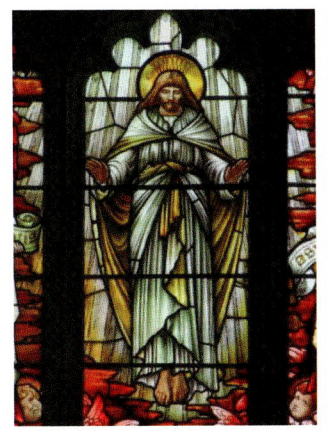

Highly individual glass  | Menorah, piscinas and sedilia  | Tablet, lectern  | The font

49

KETTON ST MARY D3, SK 982 043

St Mary from Church Road

St Mary's fame rests on the grand tower and broach spire, often quoted as one of the finest in the Midlands. The tower is a superlative example of Early English work with beautifully realised detail, the highlight being the tall and richly moulded belfry openings. Around the junction with the spire is a pretty corbel table, above which are heads. The rest of the spire soars high into the Rutland sky. The great tower and spire are held up by four massive piers with clustered shafts, these can be well observed in the crossing inside. Although the tower is Early English, the genesis of the church lies back in Norman times, if not earlier. That is best demonstrated in the typical Norman plan of central tower with transepts, flanked by the nave and chancel. The nave is aisled and there is a south porch, with a much later vestry running off the north wall of the nave. A clerestory was added in the C15th. Little Norman fabric remains, but the west entrance features a wonderful Norman doorway flanked by somewhat later pointed blind arches, all richly carved. Inside, above the arch from the south aisle to the south transept, is a curious distorted section of arch with characteristic Norman carving, from the early church. The tall arcades are Early English, with bands of nailhead in the capitals. The nave roof was reconformed at least twice, the present one is restored C15th work, previous roof lines are clearly visible on the west face of the tower. High in that same west wall is a round headed doorway, leading to a ringing floor. This is accessed through a door in the south aisle via a stairway to a passageway leading to a final unprotected open wooden stairway. The church except the chancel was restored by Sir G. G. Scott in 1861 and then the chancel itself was remade by Sir T.G. Jackson in 1863. These Victorian changes left a strangely lifeless interior, with few remaining medieval fittings. One of the best of these is the C14th font, a chunky but nicely balanced piece with Decorated window-style tracery in the panels. Some old bench ends have survived. The fashion for big, obtrusive organs in the C19th means that a nice memorial of 1594 is hidden, and another wall tablet nearby to Richard Spenser from 1723 is also hard to see clearly. The chancel roof was prettily painted in 1950, and some of the stained glass is very fine. Painted panels (C18th?) with religious subjects, including a triptych, are interesting.

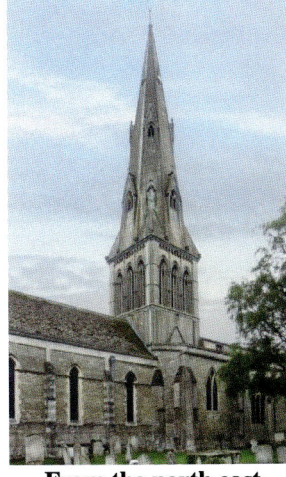

From the north east	 **Fabulous west entrance**	 **From the south west**

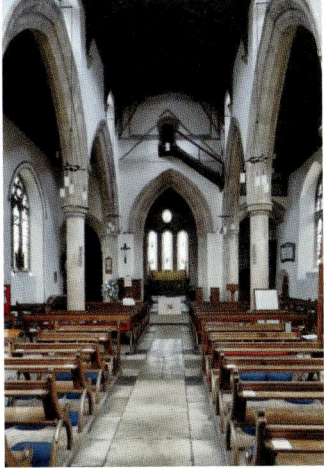

Looking east along the nave	 **Ringing floor door**	 **Looking west along the nave**	 **The chancel**

Chancel roof and angel	 **Norman carving**

The font	 **Sacred triptych**	 **Mural tablet**	 **Quality stained glass**

51

LANGHAM ST PETER & ST PAUL   A2, SK 844 112

From the extensive southern churchyard

Langham St Peter and St Paul is one of Rutland's grandest churches, both unusual in plan and attractive. Some authorities would have a Norman cruciform precursor on the site, but no structural evidence remains for that today. What is very much here today is a substantial and impressive south transept lying around 'amidships' about where a transept running off a central tower might stand, but the visitor must come to their own conclusion as to what happened here. The present transept is C14th, not Norman, but may occupy a Norman footprint. Unusually, the transept has a west aisle. A corresponding north transept stood until the early 1800's. The rest of St Peter has much to admire, too. Here again in Rutland we find a super tower and broach spire, also a high nave with aisles and a longish chancel. The C15th clerestory, in a very rare occurrence, includes two windows above the chancel arch. Most walls are crenellated, and friezes of ballflower, heads and creatures run below most of the parapets. Not least of the fine constituent parts is the south porch, once with parvise; this too is battlemented and is joined to the south aisle. The evolution of St Peter's is long and complex but the oldest parts are C13th (tower, chancel) and there was much reconfiguration through the C14th into the C15th, resulting in a decidedly Perpendicular appearance externally. The transept south window is a real Perpendicular tour-de-force. A long stable spell was broken by uninspired restoration by Christian in 1876-8, and Bodley and Garner in 1880, which included a rather bland furnishing scheme. However, the interior is light and airy, thanks to the extended clerestory and sparing use of stained glass in the windows. The stained glass that is here is notable, some of it from the hand of the iconic late C19th to mid C20th designer Sir J. Ninian Comper. The most extensive show of Comper glass is in the great transept window. Scarcely less impressive is stained glass by Frederick Preedy of 1875. Many distinctive stone heads adorn the arcades. The plain C14th sandstone font is octagonal and mounted on four pillars with a stepped base. A good incised tomb lid of 1532 resides in the transept, and there is also an old chest, but for such a fine looking church externally, the interior is a little disappointing.

From the south  | Tower/spire details 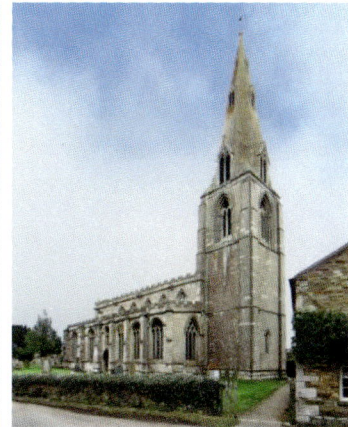 | From Well Street

Looking east and west along the church

Devotion  | Preedy glass, 1875  | The pulpit  | Springer heads

The font  | Old mortar in the porch  | Ancient chest

53

LITTLE CASTERTON ALL SAINTS D3, TF 018 099

All Saints wakes to Spring

Little Casterton village is tiny, with only one through road, and the expectation might be that the church would soon reveal itself to the visitor, but not so. It is hidden away off a small lane and can only be approached by a winding path. Is the finding worth while? Externally at least the church is rather shabby and unprepossessing, but there are many good things within, so the answer is yes. Most of the present modest building is C13th in origin and there is little outside that would indicate its true date. The plan is aisled and clerestoried nave, chancel and south porch. On the west wall of the nave sits a double bellcote with shafts, again probably an original C13th feature. Beneath that in the west wall is a lancet window. Interest will be piqued by the north doorway, which has an unadorned round arch and hints at an early foundation, but this too is thought to be C13th. It is inside that things immediately become clearer, because both arcades have round arches, and the north also has square abaci and capitals with embellished waterleaf carving, different on each capital. That indicates a date of late Norman or Transitional to Early English, i.e. C12th. More Norman evidence is provided by a tympanum salvaged from an early doorway, this depicts the Tree of Life flanked by spoked wheels. The south arcade has later features such as chamfered arches, round abaci and plain capitals and is probably early C13th. The chancel arch is similarly configured. Looking around, a wealth of intriguing features can be appreciated. In the south wall of the south aisle is a nice twin-shafted tomb recess which houses a couple of C13th coffin lids, the lower especially is highly ornate. Both splays of the west wall lancet window are painted and two female figures can be discerned, the one to the north is clearer. These are said to be early and to represent Ecclesia and Syngogia. More painting can be seen in the south aisle, but is largely indecipherable. In the chancel is a beautifully realised C13th piscina and nearby, set in the floor, is a late C14th brass depicting Thomas Burton and his wife. The nave roof is C15th and lovely, with angels on the wall battens and superb carvings on the bosses, the one of Jesus with crown of thorns is quite exquisite and full of expression. The plain octagonal font is not old, perhaps early C19th.

All Saints from the south, north and east

Looking east and west along the church

Chancel piscina   **Roof bosses and angels**   **The font**   **East window**

Tympanum, tomb recess (top); pier carving, lizard (bottom)   **Wall painting**   **Burton brass**

LYDDINGTON ST ANDREW

St Andrew from the south east

Lyddington is a most beguiling village. Its church of St Andrew and associated Bede House are two of the highlights of historical Rutland. The church is a noble, mostly C14th building, built to impress. That was doubtless due to being under the patronage of Lincoln Cathedral. The Bede House may be roughly contemporary with the church and was built as a Bishop's palace. The church plan is west tower with short spire, aisled and clerestoried nave, spacious chancel and much later vestry (of 1849) running off its north wall. There were originally north and south doorways, but both are now blocked and entrance is through a west doorway in the tower. The oldest parts are the tower and chancel, but the latter saw much reconfiguration in the C15th and C19th; the rest of the church was subjected to rebuilding during the extensive C15th programme. That resulted in the very fine nave, with its soaring arcades and large clerestory windows. An uplifting airiness is characteristic of the interior. The Victorian restoration was under the direction of Christian and Traylen in 1889-90, the chancel in particular was transformed by the removal of the wall plaster and the insertion of new furniture. However, the rare and very splendid Laudian communion rails of 1635, which form a four-sided enclosure around the altar, were spared. In accordance with the good Bishop's directions, the balusters are close enough to exclude all but the thinnest dogs. Other survivals in the chancel are a number of acoustic jars set high in the walls, and the chancel screen is C15th, although much restored. In its dado panels faint traces of the original painted flowers and figures can just be discerned. The nice sedilia and piscina appear to be C14th, but likewise, are restored. There are many other excellent features to seek out. Several areas of wall painting have been exposed although most is obscure, there is a clear figure on the north arcade next to the pulpit. It is suggested that this is Edward the Confessor. A Doom existed above the chancel arch and parts of it survive faintly on the adjoining areas of the arcades. The square font with its richly carved Jacobean cover is an unusual piece in ironstone, old but undateable. Two very good medieval brasses can be found in the floor of the chancel and in the tower are two excellent early coffin lids.

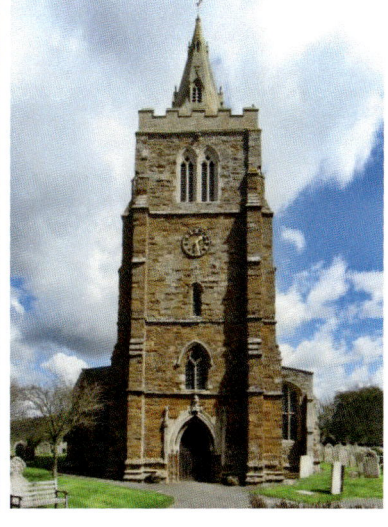

From the north and west

Looking east and west along the church **The font**

The screen **Altar and rails** **Helyn Hardy brass**

Watson brass, 1520 **Painted wall figure** **More wall painting & tablet** **Tomb lid**

57

LYNDON ST MARTIN (of Tours) C3, SK 907 044

The pleasing aspect of St Martin from the south east

Even a ruthless Victorian transfiguration could not eradicate the charm of St Martin, it remains a cheering sight when first seen from Church Road that passes off to the north east. The setting has much to do with that, in the parkland that surrounds the quintessentially English Lyndon Hall, guarded by splendid trees favoured by a variety of birds. A fabric of mellow yellow local limestone helps enormously. Contemporary reports indicate that the restoration of 1866 by T. G. Jackson was certainly needed, as St Martin was in poor shape by the early 1800's and had a history of being in bad repair. As so often, the regulation tower was spared any significant alteration during the works. It dates from the C14th, with the upper stage being rebuilt in the C15th. The rest of the church consists of clerestoried nave with low aisles with lean-to roofs, chancel, south porch and C19th organ chamber/vestry. Although the appearance is rather text-book, all is harmonious and balanced. Most if not all windows were replaced during the Victorian makeover, but the tracery of the aisle windows in particular is imaginative and attractive. The south doorway is original C13th work and the narrow south aisle, though rebuilt, is also of that date. There are hints of an even earlier Norman church, in the shape of the C12th font, which was resurrected from burial in the churchyard in 1866. The arcades date back to the church of the C13th or C14th, as do the tower and chancel arches but internally almost nothing else remains from the early church. The tower arch is notably narrow. The chancel is completely Victorian in a C14th style, fitted out with fine tiles and a superb marble reredos depicting bible stories, done in unusual graffito. The pulpit of 1866 is one to excite an opinion, if nothing else, but to the author's eyes is a splendid piece, in alabaster with dramatic red streaks. The aforementioned font has a round bowl but the top is square. It has an enigmatic ornament of hanging lobes and swirls, different on each face. Other carvings are much worn. A couple of springer heads on the arcades are very coarse rustic work. There are few mural tablets, but a benefaction plaque of 1708 has some interest. The east wall of the north aisle retains an original, but superfluous, window opening, and nearby is a rood loft opening and stairs.

From the north east  — South doorway  — From the south

Gargoyle   — Looking towards the chancel and tower arches

Altar and reredos    — Two wall tablets and a grotesque

Defunct window and rood stairs  — Jazzy pulpit  — Norman font

59

MANTON ST MARY

St Mary's highly unusual outline from the south west

St Mary is a highly individual building, a non-conformist amongst churches. Not liturgically of course, but architecturally. Whilst individual elements are conventional, together they look as if they were assembled from different boxes of parts, all resulting in a glorious melange which is quite irresistible. To begin with, the west front and double bellcote are striking C13th work, with pilaster-type buttresses, chamfered bell openings and hipped roof with two little gables each topped with a cross. The central buttress has a narrow lancet towards the base. The nave has two aisles, but the southern one is almost obscured by a considerable, originally two-storied, porch, which looks as if it has strayed from a much grander church. On its western side is a grandiose stair-turret for the upper room. Further east a short, wide transept appears, and beyond that is a large chancel, dated 1796, complete with characteristic windows, sited on the footprint of a much earlier one. Turning to the north there is another transept, rather longer and grander than the southern one, which dominates its narrow adjoining aisle. In that aisle wall is an original round-headed doorway. The north transept may have been built to house a chantry chapel in the C14th, and contains the only piscina remaining in the church, a super example of the pedestal type. The transept was rebuilt at some time later, after the C15th clerestory, because it blocks the eastern window of the latter. Going inside, oddness still prevails. The north aisle and transept have an unusual structural relationship, with the west wall of the transept continued internally to intercept the aisle in a doorway. The reason for that appears to be to create a mounting for the tomb recess that resides there. The inner arch of the recess is panelled and more traceried panelling adorns the doorway. Both arcades are round-arched and are probably part of the original church, giving a date of late C12th for its foundation. The pleasing font cannot be much more recent than the arcades, and is ornamented with a lightly carved round-arched arcade. A feature of the interior are a series of good C18th wall tablets, three of which form a family set. In the south transept is a superbly preserved C13th coffin lid, and the rustic, pillar-like poor box carries the date 1637 and the initials T.B.

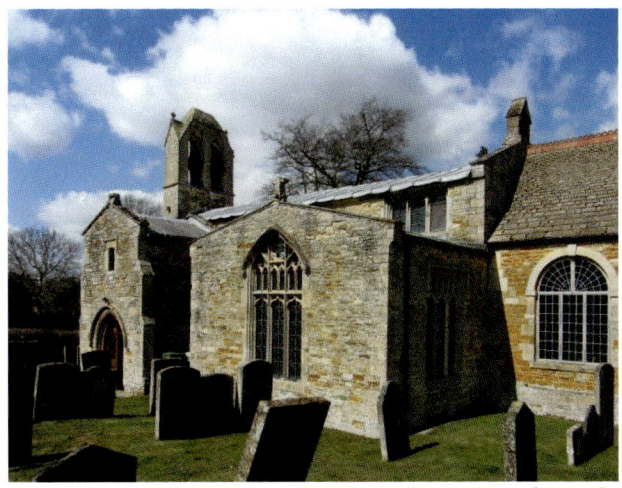

Two views from the south east and west

Sanctus bellcote, blocked window  | Looking east along the nave  | The nave through the chancel arch

A nice family set of wall tablets     | Corbels and C18[th] wall tablets

C13[th] 'omega' coffin lid  | Early C13[th] font  | 1637 poor box, initials T.B.  | Pedestal piscina, brass plate

MARKET OVERTON ST PETER & ST PAUL   B1, SK 886 165

St Peter seen in the classic three quarter view from the south west

There's a lot of ancient atmosphere around Market Overton. Especially on a bleak winter's day, the past can be felt tugging at your sleeve here in deepest Rutland. There's good reason for that, it was here that the Romans chose to found a camp, and St Peter sits within its enclosure. Later, but still a long, long time ago, the Saxons came here to build their church, maybe on the very spot where the Romans first embraced Christianity. Traces of the Romans and their artefacts turn up sometimes when the soil is turned over, and in the church of St Peter a more substantial Saxon survival stands inscrutable where it has stood for more than 900 years. This is the monolithic tower arch, its tower long gone, but echoes of it remain still in a couple of characteristic baluster shafts, probably once in a belfry opening, that now see service as supports for a stile at the churchyard perimeter. Other Saxon memories exist in three pieces of carved stone that lurk in the fabric around the base of the tower, and another carved fragment which is favoured with a place inside. Oddly, nothing remains of the Norman church that presumably followed the Saxon one, unless one counts the bowl section of the composite font, which appears to be a recycled Norman capital. The bottom section is also a reused capital, in this case an inverted Early English example. A hideously repaired break about amidships in the Norman section and encroaching green algae detract considerably from the font's appeal. Most of the present day church is from Decorated times, and consists of west tower, aisled nave, big south transept, chancel and south porch. The two smaller north transepts are Victorian add-ons housing vestry and organ chamber. The south transept is a major statement and was probably constructed as a chantry chapel. The interior is oddly characterless, which is probably the result of the Victorian restoration of 1861, but there are some worthy features to track down. The best of these is a lovely collection of C18th wall tablets, mostly housed in the chancel and thereby imparting more appeal to that area. All are large scale statements with typical embellishment in the form of cherubs, shields, cartouches, curtains being drawn aside, etc. Much more recent but nonetheless more touching is the battlefield cross for 1st World War victim Vincent S. Wing.

The church from the north and west

The nave looking towards the chancel  | From the chancel to the nave  | Saxon tower arch

Fragment of Saxon carving  | The curious font  | In memory, 2nd Lieu$^{'t}$ Wing

A fine set of C18th mural tablets

MORCOTT ST MARY THE VIRGIN

St Mary on a bitter winter's day

Rutland is blessed with a number of churches with substantial Romanesque remains, but none more so than Morcott. Inside, with a little imagination, the Norman atmosphere can still be felt. Externally, at first glance, little indication is given of the church's distant origins, but on closer examination clues begin to appear. Approaching from the west, the west face of the tower looks interesting, if rather confused. On inspection it can be seen that the doorway is Norman, with the arch butchered to accommodate a later window. Above that is an ancient niche and finally, the oddest feature of all, a gnarled, round, porthole window with several orders of framing, a bit like a folded up telescope. That too may be Norman. On proceeding to the south doorway, more Norman evidence is seen in the round arch, and to the east there is another round headed doorway into the chancel. Thus our senses are piqued for what may lie inside. But first the general layout should be assessed, it consists of west tower with short spire, short aisled nave with clerestory, chancel of roughly equal length, south porch and north organ chamber. All is built of variably coursed creamy yellow local limestone; the lower parts of the chancel walls are particularly rough coursed. The tower at some stage was subjected to a coating of stucco which is showing its age and the results of weathering. The anticipation felt when lifting the latch of any church is more than justified by St Mary's interior. Here are two splendid C12[th] Romanesque arcades, the north arcade is the older and has moulded arches, the south a little later with chamfered arches. The impressive tower arch is stylistically similar to the north arcade. As well as their beautiful arches, the arcades and tower arch also feature exuberant carving on most of the capitals, different for each pier or respond. This carving takes the form of heads of beasts and men, fluting, floriate and interlace designs, ropework and more obscure patterns. In one case two snakes are biting each other's tails. These features are undoubtedly the highlight of the interior and there are few other outstanding fittings. The font is a plain tub of indeterminate age, the pulpit and reading desk are constructed of Jacobean panels, a medieval niche houses a plain tomb and in the chancel is an excellent C17[th] wall tablet.

St Mary from the south west	The tower west face	The church from the south

Views of the C12th arcades and tower arch

The sanctuary	C12th capitals

The pulpit	The font	C17th wall tablet

NORMANTON ST MATTHEW   C3, SK 933 063

St Matthew marooned on its artificial peninsula

Now here's a church with a tale to tell! From remote rural medieval church to tourist hotspot, St Matthew has seen it all. Its fame rests solely on its history since 1970 when plans for the Rutland Water reservoir revealed that St Matthew would be inundated and lost. The planners little expected the public outcry that followed, for hadn't the church fallen out of use and been deconsecrated? But outcry there was, and a highly successful one at that. The church was saved, but at a price. Because the waves were scheduled to lap beyond the church site, the building would need special measures to ensure its survival. Those measures involved stripping the church, half filling it with concrete and then surrounding it with a protective barrier of rubble. Many purists at that point would have been happier to see the church sunk without trace than suffer such ignominy, but the plan went through and there St Matthew sits to this day, like some half sunk ship. But this ship/church is not abandoned, it now has a completely new life as a tourist and wedding venue, and is the objective of many thousands of visitors each year, most of whom walk from the large nearby activity centre and car park. Quite what the average visitor gains from that experience is a moot point, but the old church could never have dreamt of being so popular. Way back when the first building stood here, probably in the C13th or C14th, it was a humble village church and went its quiet way for some centuries until the 'big house' (Normanton Hall) and its occupants intervened. The villagers and village were cleared out of the way so as not to obstruct the view from the Hall, and Sir Gilbert Heathcote replaced the dilapidated old church in 1764. The medieval tower was retained and to it was added a plain, boxy, nave and chancel with neo-Classical windows. The old tower was taken down in 1826 when big changes were made and the west end was completely remodelled to a 'proper' Classical design, with portico, vestibule and showy tower perched above. In 1911, the rest of the church was rebuilt to create a matching nave and apsidal east end. Today the interior has been converted to a wedding venue and bears little resemblance to a church of any description, yet a visit is recommended simply to enjoy the splendid setting.

From the south east    **From the north east**

The west end    **Church and causeway**    **Tower details**

Looking east and west along the nave

Nave ceiling ornament    **Nothing of the 1764 church remains**    **Imprisoned?**

NORTH LUFFENHAM ST JOHN THE BAPTIST   C3, SK 934 033

St John from the south   **South porch**

St John the Baptist is amongst the finest of Rutland churches, a real connoisseurs building. Not only is the exterior powerful and impressive, but the interior is a veritable treasure trove of architectural interest and rare and intriguing features and fittings. Allow at least 1-2 hours to truly appreciate this fine building. The plan is of C13th west tower with a super broach spire, aisled nave, chancel and north and south porches. The clerestory, as usual, dates from Perpendicular times. The outline is blissfully free of Victorian add-ons which so often detract from a church's integrity and grace. Most of the structure is C13th to C14th, but remnants of an earlier C12th building are present in the shape of the north arcade, whose round piers have water leaf carving in the capitals. The pointed arches above are later. The south arcade is C13th, demonstrable by the busy stiff leaf carving on the capitals. The aisles are C13th and are extended to envelope the basal stage of the tower. The chancel has a low side window, provisioned most probably for the ringing of the sanctus bell on the raising of the Host. The interior walls were scraped clean of plaster in the C19th, but this normally unfortunate act here promotes a mysterious sepulchral atmosphere, which piques the excitement of exploration. The arcades retain a good show of medieval painting, with typical red colouration, and the C15th (restored) nave roof still has its original wooden angels, many with authentic colour. In the fine, big chancel are several gems, including exuberant C13th sedilia constructed in front of an earlier plain niche, a nice piscina and some splendid wall memorials, the ones to Susanna Noel (1640) and John Digby (1758) being particularly eye-catching. The latter is also commemorated with a flowing candelabrum. On the sedilia back wall is a plain brass plaque for Archdeacon Johnson (1625). In the north windows is a rare display of C14th glass, much of it, despite breakage, showing complete scenes and figures. Back in the nave an interesting C16th wall memorial of 1582, with text in both Latin and English, commemorates Simon Digby. The pulpit, though reconstructed, has original C16th panels with blank arches. The east window (c.1892) is by Kempe. The plain octagonal font is C14th.

The north frontage of St John  | Views east and west along the nave

The fine chancel  | Roof angel  | The pulpit  | C14th glass

The font | Three super wall memorials

Painted arcades  | Magnificent sedilia, and piscina  | Springer figure, capital

OAKHAM ALL SAINTS

B2/3, SK 861 089

All Saints from the south east

Tower from the north

Oakham is not a big town, but is the ideal county town for Rutland, displaying many of the facets that make the smallest county in England so distinctive – *multum in parvo* indeed. One of the best of these is the parish church of All Saints, a perfect miniature cathedral, complex in plan and evolution. Externally almost all of it appears to be Perpendicular, with all the characteristics of that period in the windows, parapets, friezes, battlements and clerestory, but in fact the church has much older roots. The tower and spire are Decorated, but even earlier is the south doorway, which is from the Early English period, i.e. early C13th. The porch that protects this doorway is late C13th. The layout has just about everything that can be put into a parish church – tower with spire, aisled and clerestoried nave, north and south transepts, chancel with north and south chapels, south porch and vestry running off the south wall of the chancel. The interior is dignified and impressive, and overwhelmingly Victorian in feel, thanks to Sir G. G. Scott's extensive restoration and refurnishing of 1857-8, but many medieval elements still exert a powerful influence. Chief amongst these are the nave and chancel arcades, which date from Decorated times and were raised later to give the high, airy ambience that enriches the interior. The capitals of the arcades are ornamented with vivacious and varied carvings, ranging from fabulous animals to grotesques and biblical scenes. The south chapel is C15th and its arcade is quite different, with battlemented capitals. The aisles and transepts have ancient roots in the C13th and the north chapel followed in the C14th, but all were later reconfigured. The transepts are divided into east and west aisles by central arcades. The roofs, though restored, have C15th origins. The chancel ceiling, especially the section above the sanctuary, is spectacular C19th work by Gilbert Scott. Many ancient stone heads pop up all around the interior, mostly associated with the arcades, but, strangely, much of the interior doesn't excite, the heavy Victorian work exercising an odd deadening effect on the 'feel'. But there is a very fine font, variously dated C12th or C13th, with typical interlinking arcading, an unattributed medieval tomb chest, five medieval piscinas, lovely late C19th reredos and excellent woodwork.

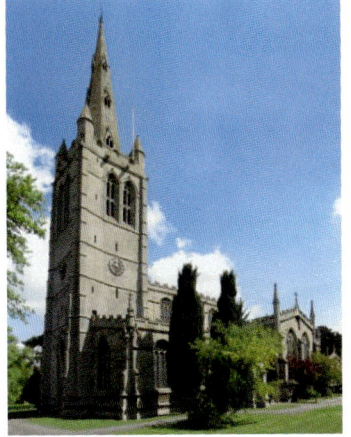

| From the south west | South doorway | Details around the south porch |

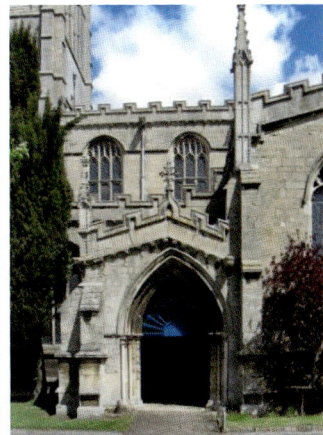

Looking east and west along the church

| The High Altar | Unidentified tomb | Piscina, north chapel |

| Capital carvings | The font | Chancel ceiling |

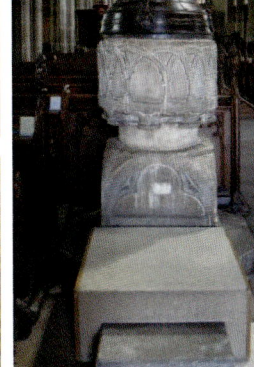

71

PICKWORTH ALL SAINTS

D2, SK 992 138

All Saints south frontage is simple, but attractive

Pickworth nestles in delectable Rutland countryside, not dramatic or stirring, but characteristic of England's heartland, with gentle hills and narrow winding roads, happily free of the clutter and rush that blights so much of our overcrowded island. Here the cuckoo can still be heard. Once the village was bigger and could boast a medieval church, but if the stories are to be believed, a battle during the Wars of the Roses decimated the village and may have seen the church wrecked. In any case, the church was a ruin by the end of the C16th. All that remains of it is a single archway from the south porch, which may or may not stand in its original place north west of the present-day church. The All Saints of today was built in 1821-2 as a result of an initiative from the then vicar of Great Casterton, Richard Lucas, who used a bequest from the will of a presumed relative, Joseph Armitage, to finance the venture. One can only suppose that the funds were not lavish, for All Saints is a very plain, severe building, housing just the bare essentials needed for a church. The style is an odd mixture of neo-Norman and neo-Classical, with no frills, but the simplicity of the design (perhaps inspired by Tickencote St Peter & St Paul) holds up well and a tour of the building, though soon accomplished, is a satisfying experience. In essence, the church consists of a rectangular box housing nave and chancel, to which is added a south porch, extended above to form a mini-tower. The windows, all alike, are of typical neo-Classical type, housed in Norman-style frames, with round heads and shafts. The doorway is similarly designed. Only the east window contains any stained glass, and this is modern, from the late 1940's. Inside, the stark interior comes as a slight shock, but the windows give excellent light and the spaciousness can be seen as an asset, highlighting what may be, in part, the original furnishing scheme of pews. The tiny internal vestry, of a piece with the pews, is quite charming, but the original three decker pulpit has gone. The square font, in keeping with the other frugal furnishings, is quite plain. A Victoria royal arms is affixed above the west window, there are two wall tablets, one for the aforementioned Joseph Armitage, a good set of altar rails and a rather nice, but defunct, old American organ.

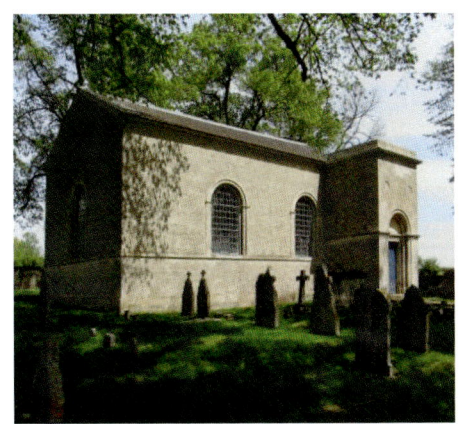

The church from the south west and south east  — Old All Saints

Looking east and west along the church  — The font

Victoria Arms  — One of only two mural tablets  — The east window

Clough and Warren organ  — The vestry

73

PILTON ST NICHOLAS

St Nicholas from the south east

St Nicholas, founded in the C13[th] or possibly C12[th], is not one of Rutland's grandest churches, and is a shy, unassuming building. That is entirely as might be expected in a shy, hidden-away hamlet deep in lovely countryside. However, like all churches, there are several points of interest which repay a keen study. The plan of nave with double bellcote and south aisle, chancel and south porch is modest and much of the exterior reflects Victorian remedial work of 1852 (chancel rebuilt) and 1878 (general restoration, porch rebuilt). However, 'round the back' on the shady north side there is a unique C15[th] window, the only one that pierces the north walls. The top portion of this consists of late Perpendicular tracery finished in red ironstone, rich in shelly fossils, with rather flamboyantly carved finials which are partly carved into the topmost element of the frame, a most unusual configuration. Nearby is a low, narrow doorway with rounded arch, now blocked, probably early C13[th]. The style of the lancet chancel windows is said to reflect the C13[th] originals. Lighting the quaint curtained-off vestry in the south west corner is a small trefoil window set in a larger splayed frame, this opening appears to be old. Inside, the visitor is greeted by a rather mundane interior with little that immediately attracts interest, but, again, like the exterior, there are some worthwhile features to be found. The Victorian chancel is attractively appointed, with a particularly fine tiling scheme on the east wall behind the altar, and good quality furnishings. The pulpit and lectern belong to the same scheme and are also well done. Of the surviving medieval elements, the font is conspicuous, but is quite plain and therefore undateable. It has a ring of columns to support the bowl, which don't appear to be a match. At the east end of the south aisle is a simple piscina, installed when that area was set aside as a chapel, possibly in the C14[th]. Nearby, set into the angle of south and west aisle walls, is a plain stone bracket, also part of the chapel fittings, which would have supported an image or statue. The arcade retains much of its C13[th] appearance, with a rounded pier and capital, with water-holding base. There is a single springer head. Various items of old stonework can be found on window sills, and there is a gravestone of 1687 against the west wall.

The church from the north east 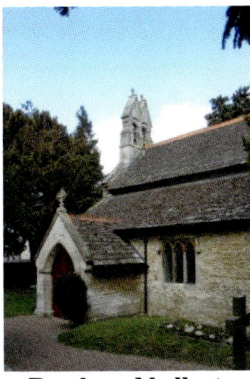 | Porch and bellcote   | North window and detail

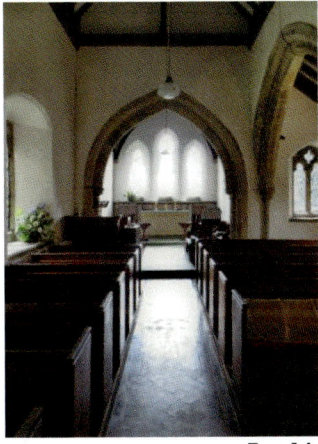

Looking east and west along the church  | The sanctuary

The pulpit  | The font  | The piscina  | St Luke tile

Capital details     | Stonework features, springer head, bracket   | Memorial and gravestone

75

PRESTON ST PETER & ST PAUL   B4, SK 870 024

St Peter hides behind its screen of cypresses

Preston lies just off the main road from Uppingham to Oakham, and is one of Rutland's prettiest villages. Its church of St Peter and St Paul is located right on the western edge of the village, with fields immediately beyond. It is a most appealing building, although it is one of those retiring churches that like to hide themselves behind a screen of trees, albeit in this case rather posh cypresses, allegedly grown from seed from the Garden of Gethsemane. The church consists of west tower with recessed spire, aisled nave, generously proportioned chancel, south porch and C19th vestry off the north wall of the chancel. Unusually, both nave and chancel have clerestories. Chapels were previously located at the east end of each aisle, the northern one is now an organ chamber. They are accessed through round arches in the chancel, which form extensions to the nave arcades. St Peter has much C13th to C14th Decorated work, but its origins go back further, into Norman times. Little of that is suspected from the outside, but it becomes immediately apparent inside in the shape of the arcades, both of which have round piers and arches. The northern one is the older, and two of its arches have smart chevron/zig-zag work; the eastern arch is later and undecorated. The central pier and west respond have square abaci and scallop carving. The south aisle is later still, and much plainer, probably dating from the early 1200's. The chancel arch is interesting and retains in its responds an unusual configuration of shafts carved with early water leaf designs. The abaci are again square, as in the north arcade. The chancel is quite opulent and has much of interest. The Caen stone reredos of 1880 is superb, with lots of high Victorian gothic motifs. Much older, and original C14th Gothic, is the lovely single sedile, its stylings echoed in the reredos. The doorway to its right is quite plain internally but outside is richly ornamented with ogee arch and finial, like the sedile, and is topped with an odd Decorated window, now with straight head and head stops. A number of archaeological artefacts including a mosaic and part of a pavement, can be found in various parts of the church. The C13th font is octagonal and plain and there are several excellent wall tablets.

Steeple and porch 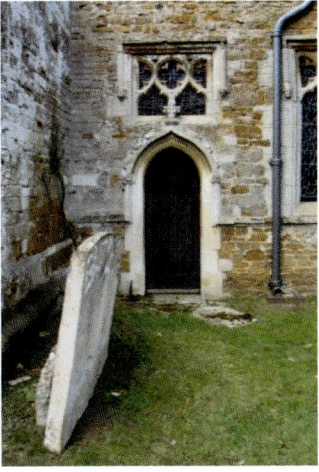   **Chancel doorway**    **The font**    **C17th chancel roof**

Looking east and west along St Peter

North arcade    **Sanctuary and reredos**    **Sedile**

Four fine wall tablets

RIDLINGTON ST MARY MAGDALENE & ST ANDREW B4, SK 848 027

St Mary from Main Street

The mainly C13th/C14th St Mary is an intriguing church, especially its position. It sits atop a quite pronounced mound that falls away quickly all around, especially towards Main Street. This configuration looks suspiciously artificial, or is perhaps a man-made modification of a pre-existing rise. In any case, it suggests that this is a very ancient site, very possibly pre-Christian. The building too is interesting, not least because of its banded appearance, created by using alternating courses of brown ironstone and pale limestone. The narrow tower doesn't seem to 'fit' and sits uncomfortably mostly within the nave, a so-called 'engaged' tower. Its position within the body of the church is a result of the steep drop in ground level immediately west of the nave. The tower east wall internally is full of oddities and seems to incorporate features of the old nave west wall, including an old roof line. The rest of the church is quite conventional, consisting of aisled nave, chancel and south porch. The north aisle is of necessity very narrow because of the sharp drop beyond down to Main Street. A rigorous Victorian restoration in 1860 saw the aisles and chancel rebuilt and a complete new furnishing scheme. Unfortunately that did nothing for the appeal of the interior and it is left to the few remaining medieval and pre-C19th features to redeem St Mary. These include the arcades and chancel arch, the former are C13th with rounded piers to the south and octagonal ones to the north. During the restoration a vigorously carved C12th tympanum featuring a griffin and lion in combat and Rutland speciality a spoked wheel was discovered. Its two halves now restored, it is resited above the vestry door at the west end. The upper section of the old rood loft stairs still survives to the north of the chancel arch, leading tantalisingly to nowhere. The other great attraction at Ridlington is a series of memorials, many to members of the Cheselden family, that noteworthy East Midlands dynasty. Some of these are striking, the earliest being a super Jacobean tablet depicting James Harington and his wife facing each other across a prayer desk. Others to Edward (d. 1688) and William Cheselden (d. 1759) are scarcely less impressive. A case containing old musical instruments is mounted north of the tower internal wall.

The church from Church Lane and the western churchyard

Views to the east and west along the nave  **At the west end**

Chancel and sanctuary  **The C12th tympanum**

Rood loft stairs  **Harington tablet**  **Tablet of 1718**  **Wm Cheselden memorial**

RYHALL ST JOHN THE EVANGELIST   E2, TF 036 108

St John from the south east

St John is an extremely likeable church, its attractions impress the visitor as soon as he or she enters the lovely, verdant churchyard. The church is set in by far the best part of Ryhall, which elsewhere is diminished by a rash of undistinguished modern housing. St John stretches comfortably in its churchyard, its Early English tower and broach spire perfectly balancing the rest of the church, which externally is mostly Perpendicular, with particularly large and graceful windows. The building consists of tower and spire, aisled nave, a grand 2-storey south porch and one of Rutland's best chancels, which has a small vestry running off its north wall. In very recent years an extension has been constructed to the north to house modern facilities. The exterior has two areas of great interest which should be explored before the church is entered. One is the scars of the site of a small building on the north aisle west wall. Few hard facts can be gleaned about this, but tradition recognises it as a hermit's cell, a hermitage. In the middle ages these were fairly common attached to churches, but were swept away at the Restoration and today few remain, or even traces of them. Here at Ryhall, a squint to the altar, the roofline, a niche and setting for an altar, survive. The other feature externally of interest is a cornucopia of corbel carvings which run all around the church on friezes and tables, with further figures as head stops. These are a most amazing and extremely vivacious collection of legendary and imaginary beasts, humanesque figures and floriate designs, one of the best to be found anywhere. Inside, there is much evidence of the early church of the C13th in the shape of stately arcades with water leaf carving in the capitals. The aisles were widened and the chancel rebuilt in the C15th, a project that included the installation of the tall windows, mostly of clear glass, which allow a beautiful lighting to permeate inside. The chancel is full of sparkling light and is beautifully furnished with many grand wall tablets and a spindly but impressive C13th double sedilia. The plain undateable octagonal font sits on a clearly unrelated base, which looks like an inverted capital of C13th date. The clerestory windows contain some old glass and the south aisle east window of around 1900 is by Kempe.

From the south   **2-storey porch**   **Chancel and sanctuary**

Looking east and west along the nave   **Arcade detail**

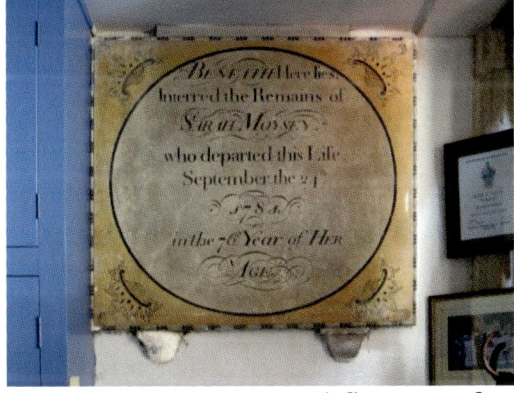

A fine array of wall tablets – 1781, 1696, 1681 and 1613

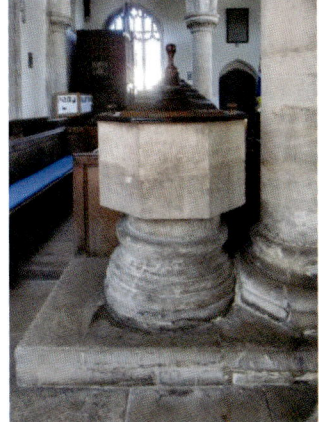

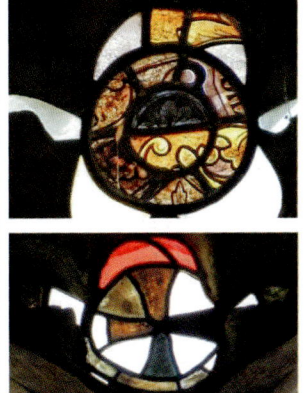

The font   **Sedilia**   **Old glass fragments in the clerestory windows**

SEATON ALL HALLOWS

All Hallows from the rolling southern churchyard

Seaton village has a population of only around 200 and is unlikely to have been much bigger in the past, so the first thing to ask oneself about All Hallows is why such a big, relatively grand, church? As in so many cases it is probably related to the influence of monied and titled local families in the middle ages and later, who would have sponsored the building and its upkeep to reflect their own status. The first church was a small Norman building, but all through the C13th and C14th this was expanded and enhanced to leave us today with a plan of tower with broach spire, aisled nave, chancel and south porch. An organ chamber, previously a sacristy and then a vestry, forms an extension to the north aisle. The spire is an interesting construction, sitting squarely atop the tower, with an extended broach section occupying half its length. Many Rutland churches have significant Norman elements, but certain of those at Seaton are likely to be amongst the earliest. These consist of the late C11th or early C12th south doorway and chancel arch responds, both of whose shafts have elaborate carvings on the capitals and abaci, many of which are fantastic and mysterious in equal measure. The south doorway has a fine round arch of many orders. Several new carvings were added to those on the chancel arch during a wide-ranging restoration in 1874-5, presumably to replace degraded originals. The church of which the chancel arch responds and south doorway formed a part was allegedly burnt down not long after it was built, and reddening on the chancel arch responds is said to derive from that fire. Both arcades are round-arched, but date from a building that replaced the earlier one, somewhere in the interval bridging the Norman and Early English periods. The north arcade has attractive alternating bands of different coloured stone in its middle and eastern arches. The interior is of purely Victorian aspect thanks to the late C19th revamp, but a few older items survive, including an excellent integrated sedilia and piscina set and three aumbries in the chancel, two tomb recesses in the south aisle (one containing a very worn effigy) with two piscinas nearby, a butchered medieval font reassembled to form a stone seat and good C18th balustered altar rails. The alabaster reredos of 1889 is a lovely piece.

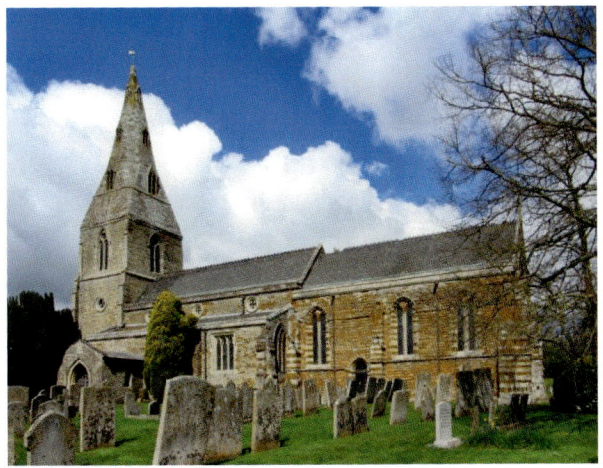

The church from the south  ..... and the north east   South doorway and details

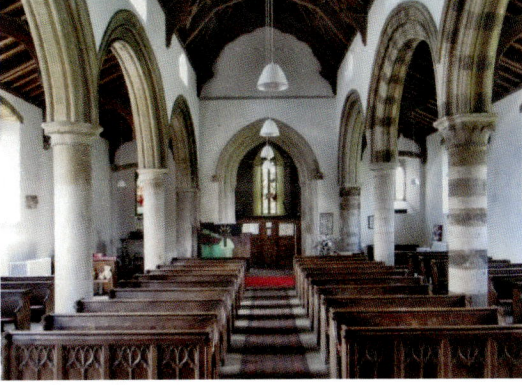

Looking east and west along the nave 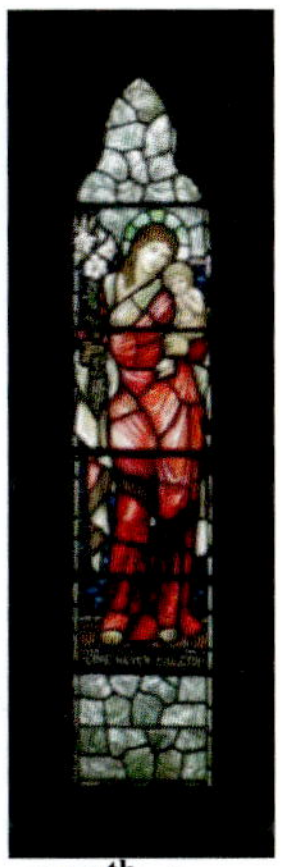 C19th glass

Chancel arch & beyond  The reredos of 1889  Font of 1875

The chancel arch carvings  C13th piscina and sedilia set

83

SOUTH LUFFENHAM ST MARY   C4, SK 941 019

St Mary from the south and its steeple

St Mary lies squeezed uncomfortably into the north west corner of its churchyard, with almost no frontage to the north and west, but such a situation does make it unmissable to all who pass by on The Street. It is a fairly unassuming, small to medium sized church with no great pretensions to grandeur, but it does have a distinctive spire. This is of the recessed type and is actually quite spindly and modest, yet nevertheless it bristles with crockets, and manages to cram three sets of lucarnes into its length, making for a fussy, but waggish, concoction. St Mary also likes to play games with photographers, and no matter how many times the building is circumnavigated, no clear view of the whole building reveals itself due to obscuring trees. The church consists of the tower and spire, aisled nave (the northern aisle being much shorter due to the loss of what was probably an eastern chapel), chancel with south chapel (now a general purpose area) and south porch. The north doorway is now unused but retains an interesting niche above. The window tracery is very low key and loosely diagnostic of the $C14^{th}$, only the replacement east window of 1852 is anything like showy. The Perpendicular clerestory extends to the chancel, adding useful extra illumination to that area. After the pleasant, yet run-of-the-mill, exterior, the interior reveals something rather grander – one of the best short Transitional Norman arcades in the county. This is the northern one, of just two bays, but the arches make a lovely sweep and the hoodmoulds contain billet moulding. Even better are the pier and responds, with their cruciform abaci and capitals fancifully decorated with volutes and heads with deadpan expressions; the east respond has water leaf. Additional nailhead decoration indicates the Transitional age. The south arcade is later and has pointed arches and waterholding bases, indicating an Early English age. The list of worthy internal fittings is not a long one, but there is a good $C14^{th}$ tomb with effigy in the chancel, triple sedilia nearby, $C14^{th}$ font with quatrefoils on the bowl, a bucolic head below the west respond of the arch to the old chapel, $C14^{th}$ piscina in the old chapel and a most unusual and attractive stone pulpit of c.1861. The few wall tablets are unexceptional. Restorations in 1852 and 1861.

From the east  — **North doorway and niche**  — **North arcade**

Pier detail and head   — **Looking east and west along the nave**

Sedilia   — **C14th tomb in chancel, and its effigy**

The font  — **Pulpit and lower portion of old screen**  — **Wall tablets**

85

STOKE DRY ST ANDREW

Lichen is taking over St Andrew's ancient walls

Allow plenty of time to explore St Andrew, there is an awful lot to take in. This small, modest church in a quiet corner of Rutland contains a quite amazing number of fascinating survivals. The exterior of St Andrew is undistinguished apart from an inherent antique charm, and a grand north porch of the Tudor period, with top storey and rare oriel window topped with battlements. The component parts are thin west tower, aisled nave, chancel and adjoining south chapel, and north and south porches. The south chapel boasts its own gabled roof, and makes a feature to the east with the chancel. The early church was Norman, demonstrated by short lengths of string course with saw-tooth moulding, but most of the building dates from the C13th and C14th with a flourish of activity in the late Perpendicular, which resulted in the north porch and clerestory. Victorian changes are scarcely noticeable, but the fine pulpit dates from that period. Thus, the interior looks and feels extremely ancient, a feeling reinforced by the features and fittings. The first thing that draws the eye on entering and looking east is the screen to the chancel, a partially complete C15th example, very rare in Rutland. Note especially the elaborate coving, which survives along the top. The chancel is wonderful, filled with good things. Two shafts supporting the arch are Norman and are covered with vibrant carvings of beasts, humans, foliage, bells and much more, the whole alive with activity. Either side of the east window are C14th wall paintings, St Andrew being crucified to the left plus more enigmatic subjects, and to the right what may be a scene at an altar, or the Virgin Mary on a throne, but this painting is not easy to interpret. To the right of the altar is a super late C16th tomb, for Kenelm Digby and his wife. The altar rails are classic C17th. In the south chapel is another Digby tomb of the mid-C16th with much abused effigy, and a fabulous C13th wall painting showing St Christopher and King Edmund, very clear following restoration. Other wall paintings adorn the chapel and there are C16th examples on the clerestory walls. Yet another tomb (late C15th) in the south aisle has a badly-preserved incised alabaster lid. Some bench ends are C16th and have contemporary poppyheads. There is much more in this must-visit church.

St Andrew from the north east 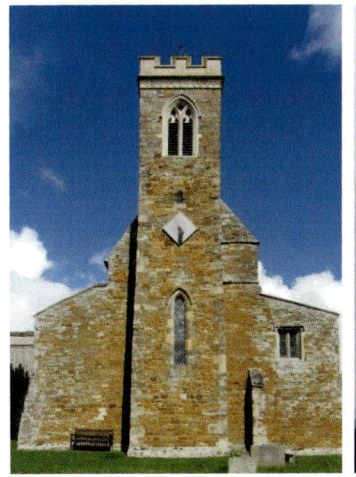   **…. and from the west**    **Jaqueta Digby d. 1496**

Looking east and west along the church

A great deal of interest in the chancel    **Kenelm & Anne Digby tomb**    **C16th poppyhead**

Chancel east wall paintings    St Edmund & St Christopher      **Chancel arch shafts carvings**

STRETTON ALL SAINTS   C1, SK 950 158

All Saints from the north west

All Saints lies on the southern edge of Stretton at the end of a narrow lane. The church consists of nave with western bellcote, north aisle and north and south transepts, chancel and south porch. It is defended by a small army of trees that surround the fairly restricted churchyard. The evolution of the building is interesting, there is very old work like the Norman south doorway to mark the church's origins, and much of the main fabric is not much younger. Early English lancet windows are dotted around the building, and the north aisle and its much-admired arcade are also of that age, as is the chancel. The bellcote and south porch are C13th. One intriguing possibility is that the round, primitive Norman arch to the south transept is the original arch to the original chancel, transferred to the transept when it was built at the same time as the chancel was rebuilt with a new arch. The north transept is thought to be late C13th in age. Later changes saw new windows fitted in the chancel in the C14th and C15th, and the south transept was rebuilt with a flat-topped late Tudor style window some time before the C18th. Inevitably and apparently by necessity, there was a fundamental rebuilding and refitting in 1881, at which point the building was in a sorry state. Highlights of the interior include the arcade, which has round arches and elegant four-shafted pier and responds with fine stiff-leaf carving in the capitals, and some excellent C13th features in the chancel including a simple but beautifully conceived double-arched piscina, next to which is a decorous recess with many-moulded pointed arch, hoodmould and head stops. The stone seat beneath the arch may replace an original tomb, in order to create sedilia. Two original image brackets survive either side of the altar. Another image bracket can be found in the south east corner of the north transept, associated with a small piscina. These were doubtless connected with the use of the transept as a chapel. The south transept almost certainly performed the same function. In this transept are two good mural tablets of the early C18th; another C18th tablet with marble backplate can be found in the chancel. The font is square and solid, with moulded, engaged shafts at the corners, it may be from the original church. Two old benches reside in the transepts.

| From the south east | North side & Wilson memorial | South doorway |

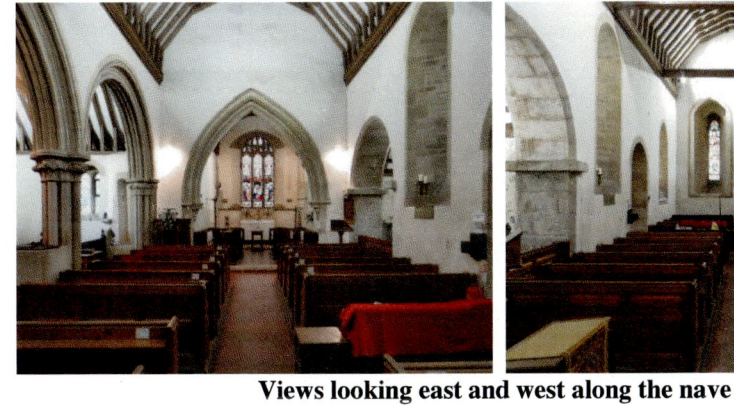

Views looking east and west along the nave  | The font

| The sanctuary and altar rails | Piscina and tomb? recess | Bracket, piscina, rood opening |

| Chancel arch respond | Memorial tablets (c.1720, c.1714) |

TEIGH HOLY TRINITY   B1, SK 865 160

Holy Trinity from the north west

Now here's something different in the pantheon of Rutland churches, a building very largely constructed in 1782. One source states that a fire precipitated the rebuilding of the original C13th/C14th medieval church, but whatever the reason, only the lower portion of the tower remains from that building. This is of roughly coursed ironstone rubble, whilst the 1782 parts are of limestone ashlar. The style is Gothic Revival but a rather unimaginative version, at least externally. The nave and chancel are contained under one roof in a rectangular box with battlements, odd stumpy pinnacles and a frieze adding touches of individuality. The original 1782 windows were of plain glass without tracery; in the late C19th they were replaced with Decorated style versions with stained glass. The tower has a south doorway and a west doorway, the latter is the main entrance to the building and opens into a circular vestibule beneath the tower. All the good things are found inside, and it is a thrilling surprise when after the gloom of the vestibule one emerges into a quite remarkable interior. Ahead lie two banks of box seating, facing each other across the church, a classic 'collegiate' arrangement. The reason for that soon becomes clear, because the pulpit is located, highly unusually, at the west end. Thus, by having the seating facing north and south, the congregation are able to turn their heads easily between the altar and the pulpit. The pulpit is configured as a grandiose double-decker affair, with high central section from which the priest delivers the sermon, and a lower tier with two matching desks for the reader and the clerk, all built up against the west wall. These eyries are approached via narrow, awkward stairs. Behind the upper tier is a trompe l'oeil window, with painted trees masquerading as an outside view. All in all, a quite amazing set-up. Behind the altar in the tiny sanctuary is a painting of the Dutch School dated around 1600, of the Last Supper. The sanctuary is protected by neat iron railings. There are two fonts, one much admired, the other, not. The former is a delicate Georgian mahogany bowl, elegantly ornamented and shaped, the other an inexpert example carved by an incumbent in the mid-C19th. Lord's Prayer, Creed and Decalogue boards are located on the west and east walls.

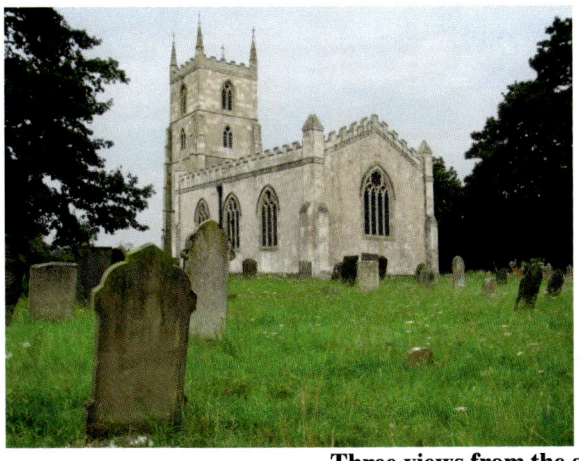

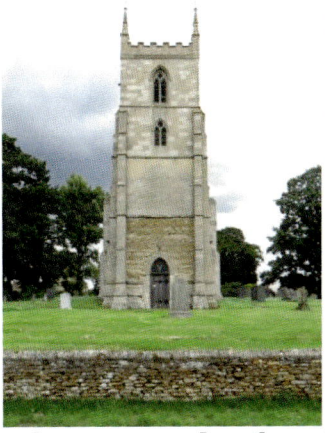

Three views from the south east, west and south west

Looking east and west along the church

The pulpit at the west end    Sanctuary and painting    Doorway into the vestibule

The two fonts    Late C19th stained glass    George III arms on the ceiling

THISTLETON ST NICHOLAS   C1, SK 913 180

View from the south east, showing the distinctive chancel

When approached from the west St Nicholas appears at first glance to have a fairly standard layout, but when the east end and the highly distinctive chancel is seen, it is clear that this is anything but a conventionally designed church. In fact, only the tower remains of the medieval church, the rest is the result of a thorough rebuilding in 1879-80 by the incumbent of that time, the Revd J. H. Fludyer. Tragically his three young children died within a few weeks of each other of scarlet fever in 1841-2, and he rebuilt the church as a memorial to them, although why that wasn't done until 1879 is a mystery. That wasn't the first rebuilding of St Nicholas, an antecedent of the good reverend, the MP Sir George Bridges Brudenell, rebuilt the nave (at the very least) in the 1780's. All of that work has now been overprinted, although possibly the rubble north wall of the nave remains. The plan is simple – tower, nave and chancel with south porch and north organ chamber/vestry off the chancel. The 1879 nave is undistinguished, but the chancel is something of a minor High Victorian tour-de-force. Externally it is a half-octagon, which internally becomes a semi-circle, whose fittings include terracotta saints in niches and a lovely terracotta reredos. A frieze of improving texts runs around the top of the stark walls of smooth limestone ashlar. The atmosphere is reminiscent of a Greek temple. A rose window is set due east flanked by two lancets. Externally, there is an elaborate frieze of leaves and ballflower, and alarming gargoyles loom from the angles. The ashlar-clad tower also has gargoyles of an earlier vintage. The round pulpit belongs to the chancel furnishing scheme and is a most unusual piece, again in smooth limestone with two decorative bands at the top and texts around the middle; it is approached from the chancel via a stone doorway with an impressive ogee headed arch. The church floors are of Minton tiles. The walls are notably bare, with only one white marble wall tablet, again for the Fludyer children. This is hidden away under the tower. There is a brass wall plate on each of the piers of the chancel arch. The font is plain and presumably part of the 1879 furnishing scheme. Immediately north of the church are the lovely C17th/C18th Old Rectory and barn.

From the west	The chancel	Chancel exterior detail

Looking east and west along the church	The sanctuary

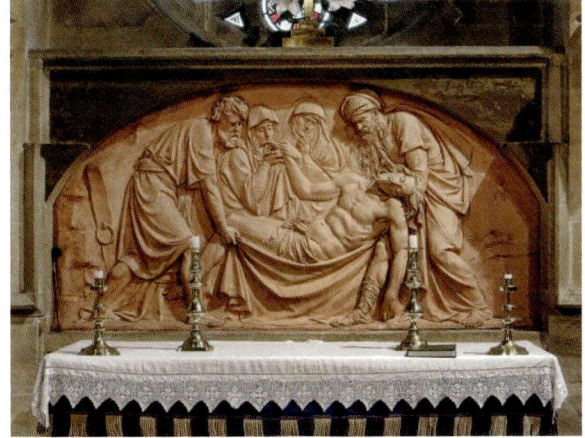

Terracotta reredos - the Entombment	Chancel roof	The pulpit

The font	Fludyer tablet and plate		Oil lamp

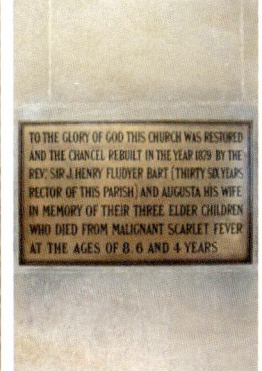

93

TICKENCOTE ST PETER D2, SK 990 095

St Peter from the north west

Tickencote St Peter is probably the best known and possibly the most visited church in Rutland (with the exception of Normanton and Oakham). Church lovers get very excited about the building, with good reason, yet amongst the admiration for some wonderful and rare late Norman fabric, the keen observer probably won't escape a hint of disappointment. For a start not much of St Peter is Norman at all, it was almost entirely rebuilt in 1792 on the orders of an enthusiastic, and presumably very rich, local churchgoer, Miss Eliza Wingfield. The architect was Samuel Cockerill. Clearly the church was in a very poor state, yet there is reason to believe that a great deal of, perhaps serviceable, Norman fabric was in place. Regardless of that, the Cockerill rebuilding was drastic. Very likely, much that would be of inestimable value today was disposed of. It is debateable how much of the old plan was followed in the rebuilding, but old drawings do not show an exterior much like the one we have today, with the exception of the east and chancel walls. The old St Peter consisted of nave and chancel, with a bellcote at the junction of nave and chancel. Cockerill's rebuilding introduced a substantial south porch, extended upwards as a tower, and a corresponding north vestry which fundamentally changed the morphology of the church. Yet the new church, if taken purely on its merits, is actually an intriguing building that despite the intention to make it look Norman, cannot avoid looking Classical too. But it is inside that Tickencote keeps all its trump cards, and the first of these hits the visitor in the face as soon as they enter. This is a stunning late Norman chancel arch, with five orders of amazing carving, seemingly completely out of place in a small church in a hamlet in darkest rural England. The smallness of the building makes it seem even larger than it is, and the question always lingers – why is it here? Beyond it, the chancel was rebuilt more or less as it was before, and there is no doubting the ancient and sepulchral feel within, reinforced by the mid-C12th vaulted roof and its central boss, perhaps the earliest of its kind in the country. In the south wall is a recess containing a battered wooden effigy of great age. The nave is all work of 1792, but contains a very fine Transitional Norman font.

The church from the south  | Tower and integral porch  | Details of the porch arch

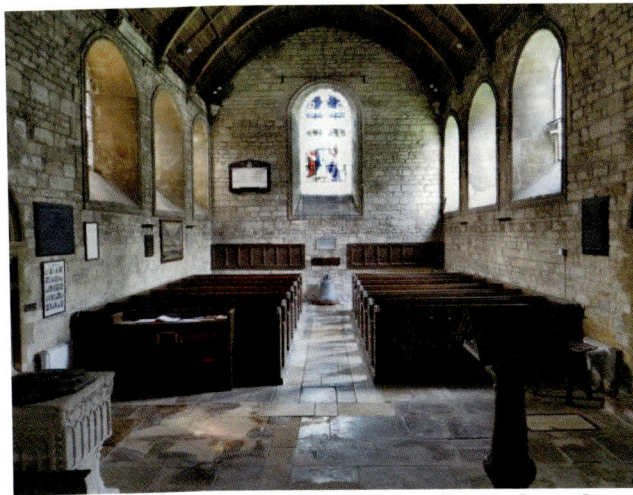

Looking west and east along the nave, and the amazing chancel arch

Chancel arch detail 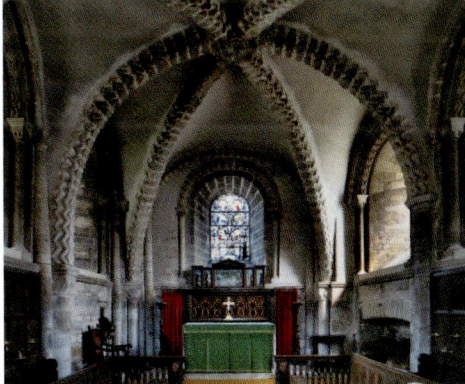 | Chancel and vaulted roof  | The central boss

The wooden effigy  | The font  | Terrible twins

95

TINWELL ALL SAINTS   D3, TF 006 064

The church from the south

All Saints may have evolved from a Norman predecessor with a simple nave and chancel plan. Despite some claims that the distinctive saddleback tower is also partly Norman, there is no evidence for that. It probably dates from an extensive rebuilding in the C13th which also included a restructured chancel and south aisle. A north aisle was also built at some stage in the C13th or C14th but this was later absorbed into the nave and the arcade removed. That was probably done in the C15th, at a time when the old north aisle wall was rebuilt and raised, and a clerestory put in. The nave roof now embraces the area of the old north aisle. Also in the C15th the chancel was rebuilt, but the old chancel arch, with its stylish stiff leaf ornament in the capitals, was retained. A small, but clearly ancient, two-arch piscina-like moulding now reset below the east window may also originate from the C13th chancel. The windows largely date from the C15th rebuilding programme although there are two original C13th lancet windows with dogtooth moulding in the arches, and also some with flattened heads which have a C16th look to them. A far-reaching restoration in 1849 introduced the staid Victorian fittings and the very strong atmosphere of the C19th inside. Despite that there is more to All Saints interior than might be expected, and the list of interesting items is a fairly long one. Firstly there are several wall tablets ranging from the C17th to the C19th and also a super monument of c.1611 in the chancel which is usually described as being typical of the style of the Renaissance. It takes the form of a large, ornate tablet with ionic columns to the side and finials on the flat top, with three prominent shields in the centre. Near the altar is a wordy Victorian tablet commemorating two bastions of the empire who fell in service overseas. Also in the chancel are a sadly deteriorated tablet of 1668 and two restrained C18th tablets. Two more flowery C18th tablets adorn the nave. Other lesser tablets are dotted around. A squint looks through to the altar from the south aisle. An amusing bellringers rhyme lurks beneath the tower. Above the chancel arch is an unusual George I arms in plaster. Typical Victorian fittings include the font of 1893 and carved figures of the Evangelists on bench ends at the front of the nave.

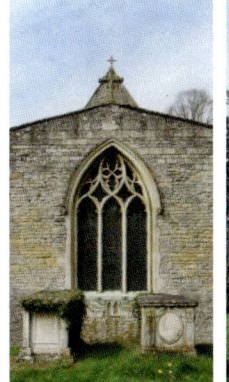

All Saints from the south east, east and north

Looking east and west along the nave

| The chancel | South aisle squint | Bellringers rhyme |

| Elizabeth Cecil monument | George I arms | Amey Cave tablet | Font of 1893 |

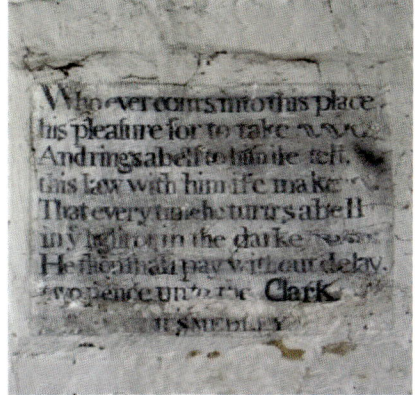

TIXOVER ST LUKE

St Luke from the south

One of Rutland's most atmospheric churches, St Luke lies way apart from its tiny village, tucked in close to the River Welland and the Northamptonshire border. There isn't a house or building anywhere near, St Luke appears, like a mirage in the fields, as the visitor slogs the mile or so along the rough track from civilisation. But make sure you undertake the walk, because St Luke is not to be missed, if only for the highly charged and slightly eerie 'feel' of the setting. Once it had a village to keep it company, but that migrated away from St Luke many centuries ago. Quite a lot of an original C12th building survives, mainly in the form of the very fine Norman tower – chunky and solid with fascinating detail in the bell openings and odd lonely window in the second stage on the south side. The marvellous tower arch with its five shafts on each side and mysterious capital carvings is also Norman, as is the font. An ancient round-headed doorway above and to the left of the tower arch appears to be contemporary with it. Almost all the rest is C13th, a rebuilding of the original structure, but the high, short nave must surely sit on the old ground plan; the chancel is longer and rather more typical of C13th work. All the windows, except those of the clerestory, are simple rectangles with one to three lights; the jury is out as to whether these are C13th or later C16th/C17th replacements. The round clerestory windows (south side only) are small and Victorian, and totally inadequate to light the very dark interior. The complex south doorway has both C12th and C13th features, its porch is a century or two later. The south arcade has round arches, but Early English detail; as in many cases in Rutland, the old Norman architectural ideas were practised here into the C13th. The north aisle and its arcade are somewhat later, but still C13th, the pier has very good stiff leaf carving. The old rood loft steps wind up to a higher doorway from this aisle. There are a few minor C18th and C19th wall tablets dotted about, but the outstanding memorial in St Luke is the riotous monster in the chancel for Roger Dale, d. 1623. One small piece of English and three sections of continental C16th/C17th glass are emplaced in the south aisle window. Some pews may be Jacobean and there is a manorial box pew in the south aisle. The white stone pulpit is of 1859.

Views from the north and south east  **Norman tower window**

Views east and west along the church  **The tower arch**

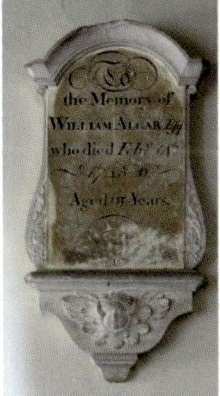

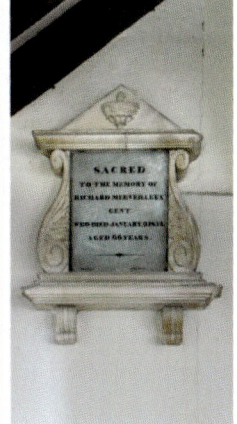

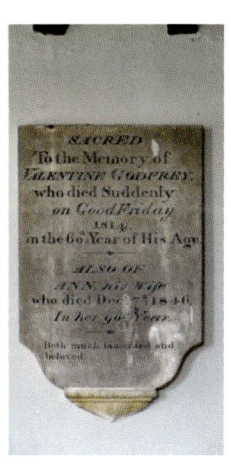

Details of the arcades and tower arch **Three wall tablets**

Roger Dale memorial  **The font**  **C17th Swiss glass**

UPPINGHAM ST PETER & ST PAUL   B4, SP 867 996

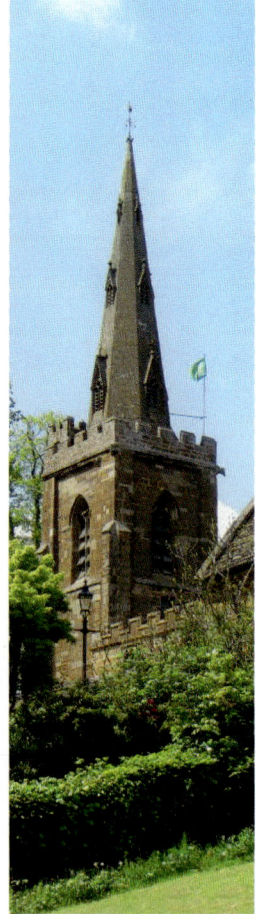

St Peter & St Paul from the south east   **The steeple**

St Peter is a town church in every sense, it sits right in the heart of Uppingham, nestled amongst the other essential amenities of this charming place. The north entrance porch is accessed directly from the market place. On the south side the churchyard falls away abruptly into a narrow valley, and presents a quite different aspect. The building consists of west tower and spire, nave with aisles extended onto the chancel to house a north chapel and south organ chamber/vestry, chancel and north and south porches. Like many town churches the largely C14th St Peter was particularly enthusiastically restored in the C19th (1860-1 by Henry Parsons) and the interior especially was fundamentally reconfigured. Amongst much building work, the chancel was completely rebuilt, the nave extended eastwards and many galleries removed. A classic Victorian furnishing scheme was installed and suitable devotional pall imposed. Even now a citizen of 1880, for example, would feel quite at home here. Some medieval items survived the onslaught, but most of these take some finding. The most intriguing and important are the smallest, these are four carved stones of clearly very ancient origin, found during restoration. Two are mounted either side of the chapel east window, and the others either side of the north door. They may be broken but retain details down to the waist of four figures. They are loosely dated as Norman, but would surely originate from early in that period. They are superbly carved and the figures are full of vitality, they depict two figures giving blessings, one of whom, at least, might be a bishop, and two angels. They almost certainly originate from the first church built here. The elegant arcades and tower arch remain from the C14th church. The plain, octagonal, medieval font has recently returned triumphantly to the nave from under the tower, with its Victorian forerunner dispatched to Uppingham School chapel. A medieval painting scheme can be discerned on the south arcade arches. The pulpit is a dignified, somewhat reconstructed C17th example. The marble and Caen Stone reredos is simply superb and the Moorish arcades in the chancel are a nice exotic touch. Above them golden angels glow attractively, in contrast to their dark sisters who repose in the gloom of the nave roof.

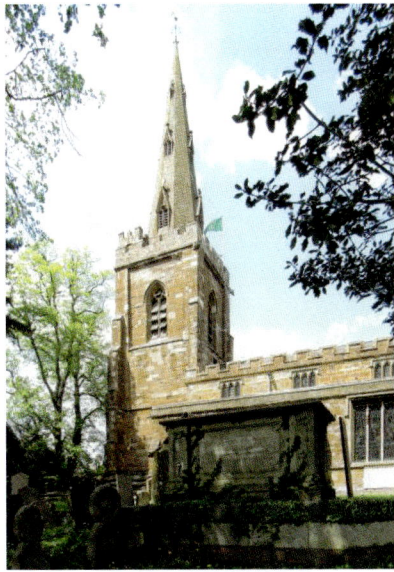

In the churchyard    **South aisle, west end** 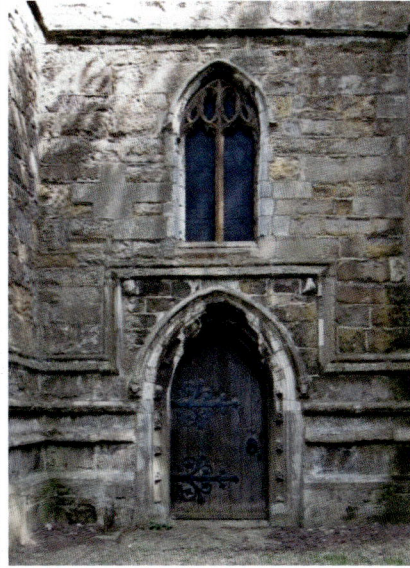   **West doorway through the tower**

Views east and west along the church    **Chapel arch**

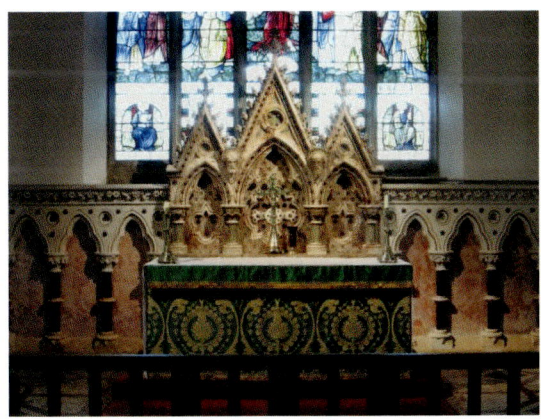

Beautifully furnished sanctuary    **The font**    **The pulpit**    **Chancel roof angel**

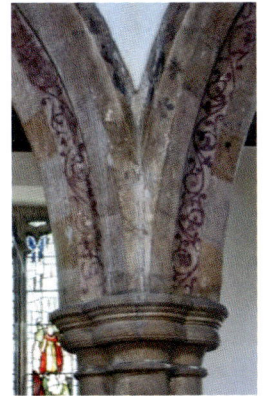

South arcade painting      **Three of the four Norman carved figures**

101

WARDLEY ST BOTOLPH   A4, SK 832 002

St Botolph from the south

The struggle to retain St Botolph as a working church finally ended in 2010, when it was declared redundant. Wardley is a hamlet with less than 50 inhabitants and the financial burden was too great, but some of the villagers still determinedly keep the old building shipshape. Not just shipshape but clean, tidy and ready for a service at any time. All credit to them, it is a pleasure to visit this venerable church, which enjoys a grand position on its small mound. The layout is very simple, just west tower and broach spire, high, short nave with clerestory, south porch and a very incongruous chancel of 1871. The nave is the oldest unit of the church and has a late Norman south doorway, quite a modest example in a county that has several crackers, but with the same Romanesque solidity and confidence. To its left is an Early English lancet window and to its right is another style of window from the C13th, one that is quite rare in Rutland, of plate tracery design. Low down near the junction of the nave and chancel is a small square window of later date. Above these is a three window clerestory, which is repeated on the north side, but oddly there are no other windows on that side. However, there is a blocked doorway, again of Romanesque type. The chancel also lacks north side windows, and has only one on the south side, of Decorated affinities, said to be 'modern' i.e. Victorian, but it shows a lot of weathering and looks much older. The east window may be a reused C15th example. The tower and spire are C14th. The interior is very plain and whitewashed, which imbues everything with an antiseptic brightness. Sadly, the whitewash was extended to cover four very old head stops on the arch and hoodmould of the tower arch, rendering their details difficult to discern. There are no great memorials or objects within, in fact the interior is rather stark, and a round-up of the features and fittings is soon accomplished. The font, in keeping with everything else, is small, plain and unadorned save for the date 1797. Nearby on the north nave wall are Victorian commandment, Lord's Prayer and Creed boards. The furniture may mostly be contemporary with the font. A few second division mural tablets enliven the uniform whiteness of the walls. A rare Victorian barrel organ stands near the chancel arch.

From the south west  | South doorway  | From the north east

Views looking east and west, and the tower arch

Sanctuary and east window    | Three wall tablets  | The font

Around the chancel arch    | Three strange denizens of the parish

103

WHISSENDINE ST ANDREW
A2, SK 833 143

St Andrew from the south west

St Andrew is a powerful statement in stone, big and assertive yet graceful at the same time. In a county where there is an alluring church around every corner, this is one of the finest. Much of that is attributable to the noble C14th tower, tall, strong and stylish with a grand belfry stage with long elegant openings, both open and blind, with recessed mouldings. The west front is scarcely less impressive and features in the lower stage a tall, refined arch of three receding orders. This archway extends upwards for the full height of the first stage of the tower and encloses a doorway with window above. Above this in the second stage are three empty niches. The rest of the church consists of aisled nave with clerestory, chancel with transepts, big south porch and a Victorian vestry on the north side of the chancel. There is some C13th work, but mostly the church fabric dates from the C14th and C15th. The clerestory has a lovely row of six Perpendicular windows each side and the other windows are large and mostly of the same period; the north transept has an attractive Decorated north window. The interior is filled with light thanks to the clerestory and big windows, and one's first impression is of space and a cathedral-like atmosphere, courtesy of the high nave and lovely flowing C13th arcades. The chancel is largely Victorian work following a major refurbishment in 1865-70, but has high quality fittings like the east window with glass by Kempe and a very handsome reredos. A nicely restored tablet with Sherard achievement commemorating the rebuilding of the chancel in 1640 enhances the north wall, with an amusing touch afforded by the dog's tail being carried beyond the frame on the right. There are a few nice memorial tablets in the church, the best being the one for Bennett and Dorothy Sherard in the south transept. Up in the nave roof are a series of seated wooden wall plate figures which are mounted on lower crouching figures; presumably these two types are associated with different phases of roof building. The C14th font is odd, only four of its eight sides are fully carved, the others are just superficial sketches. An old, ornate screen ex-of St Johns College, Cambridge divides off the south aisle from the south transept. Two broken C13th coffin lids lie in the north aisle.

From the south and west — **Top stage of the tower**

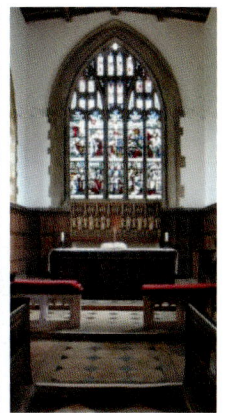

Looking east and west along the church — Sanctuary & east window

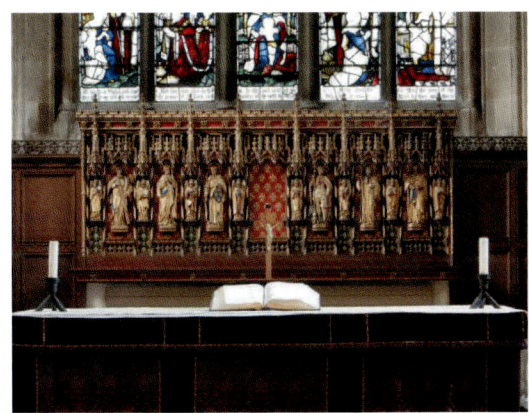

The reredos — **Kempe glass** — **The font** — **South transept piscina**

Wall post figures — **Springer figures** — **Sherard achievement** — **C18th wall tablet**

WHITWELL ST MICHAEL   C3, SK 924 088

From the south west

Whitwell was once a quiet little spot, tucked away in darkest Rutland and minding its own business. To some extent, that is still true, but now, with Rutland Water just a few hundred metres away with its leisure facilities and car parks, and a seething main road through the hamlet, nothing will ever be quite the same again in this corner of the county. St Michael though goes serenely on, ticking off the years of yet another century, and it has seen a great many since a C12th (or perhaps even C11th) church stood here. Little or none of that remains now, but much of the fabric is C13th and a real antique feel envelops the building. St Michael is one of Rutland's smallest churches, and its plan is modest, consisting of nave with bellcote and south aisle, chancel and south porch. The C13th double bellcote may be amongst the oldest in the county and the south aisle is also C13th. Also the south doorway, which has a round arch, thin shafts with rings and nailhead in the capitals. There was much restoration work and alteration in the C14th, and the Victorian restoration came in 1881. As a result of the latter, the interior furnishings are mostly C19th. A feature of the interior is the inordinate number of piscinas for such a small church, no less than four. As well as the customary one in the chancel, the other three mark the locations of chapels at the east and west ends of the aisle, and the east end of the nave. The one at the east end of the aisle has a small aumbry (?or niche) for company, and the one in the chancel, a single sedile. The chancel has unusual friezes or cornices, C14th century or perhaps earlier, with ballflower, dogtooth, flowers and heads. At the foot of the chancel north wall by the altar is an empty recess, and beneath the altar (and elsewhere in the chancel and also the nave) are several floor slabs, the oldest of which are C17th. The panelled wood pulpit is mostly Jacobean and rests on a modern stone base, the nice balustered altar rails are also C17th. The late C12th font is a curiosity, once square, it has seen its corners roughly chamfered to create a crude octagon, which action resulted in the butchering of the stylised ornament. In the chancel one of the windows has a rare section of C14th glass depicting the crucifixion, supported by other random pieces. The ancient parish chest survives in the nave.

St Michael from the south and south east  **South doorway**

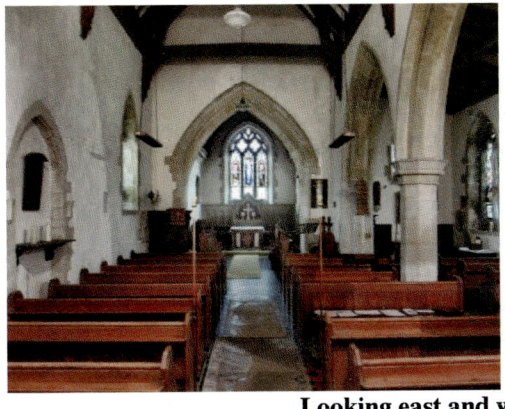

Looking east and west along the church 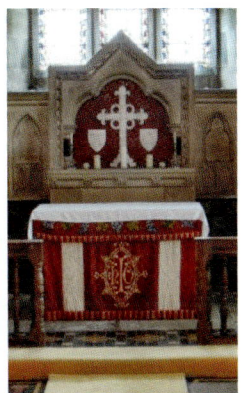 **Altar and reredos**

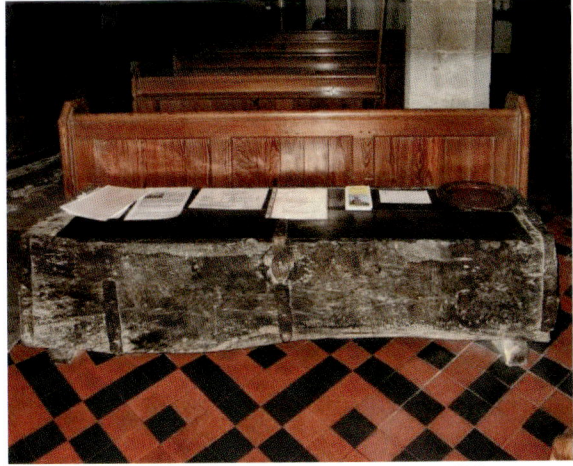

Ancient parish chest (modern lid) 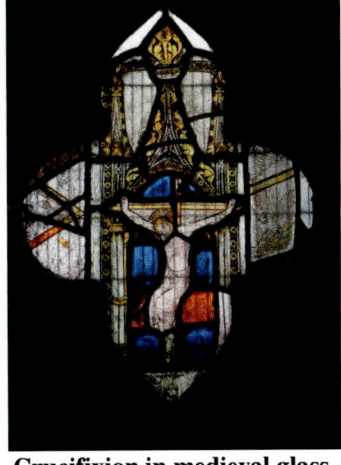 **Crucifixion in medieval glass**  **The font**

Pulpit & piscina  **Piscina & aumbry, south aisle**  **Wall painting** 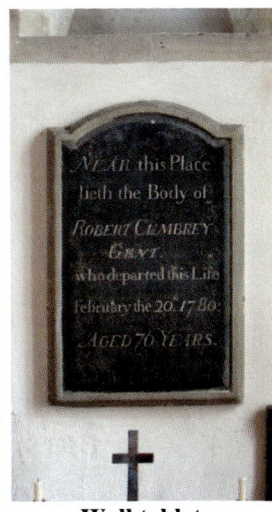 **Wall tablet**

WING ST PETER & ST PAUL

B4, SK 894 030

From Top Street in Wing

Wing is a delightful village and pride of place in its attractions belongs to St Peter & St Paul, beautifully situated on a rise off Top Street. Architecturally it is quite a busy building, and in addition to the usual west tower, aisled and clerestoried nave, chancel and north porch, there are Victorian additions in the shape of a north chancel aisle for the vestry and an adjoining transept for the organ. With time, these have blended in nicely with the older parts. In fact the whole of the chancel is a $C19^{th}$ rebuild of a $C13^{th}$ original, and dates from 1875. The origins of the church go right back to the $C12^{th}$, from which century date the round-headed north doorway with its ringed shafts, and both arcades. Of the latter, the south arcade is the oldest, dating from the middle of the $C12^{th}$. It has cylindrical pillars and big, square abaci with scalloped capitals. The later north arcade is from the end of the $C12^{th}$, and has octagonal abaci and odd, long water leaf-like carvings on the capitals. The original $C12^{th}$ aisles were rebuilt and/or modified later, and the south aisle was rebuilt as part of a restoration in 1885. The piers of the south aisle rest on stubs of the original nave wall of the first church. Both arcades have round arches, the southern one has lozenge ornament on all but the half arch which abuts the tower. The north arcade is unadorned. East of the south arcade, high in the wall, is a rood loft opening. It is suggested that St Peter had a bellcote until the late $C14^{th}$, when it was replaced by the present tower. Lack of space resulted in the tower being set partly into the nave, and the west arch of both arcades is truncated at mid-point, dying into the tower east wall. There was a spire until around 1840 when it was removed as unsafe. Inside, apart from the ancient arcades, the feel is very much Victorian, but there are some good things to seek out. The font is plain and eight-sided. It appears to be old, and $C14^{th}$ might be the best guess for its age. An ancient altar slab, probably dating from the very first church, is now restored to its rightful place; it has five clearly marked crosses. There are a few old heads to find, some tucked away in unlikely places. In vestry windows are two small medieval roundels of painted glass. The piscina and sedile in the chancel are $C14^{th}$ and were reset when it was rebuilt. The few wall tablets are worthy of inspection.

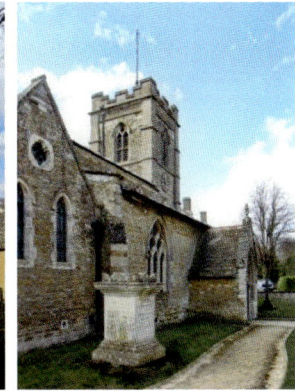

St Peter & St Paul from the north west, south east and north east

Looking east and west along the church — South arcade & rood doorway

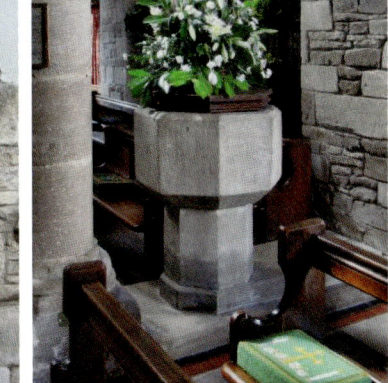

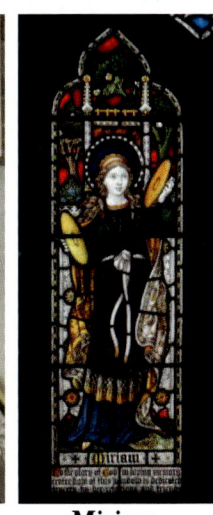

Rood doorway — The font — Piscina & sedile — Miriam

Heads — Altar consecration cross — C18th wall tablet — Arcade capitals

109

References and Select Bibliography

Rutland churches have long been recognised as important historical buildings, reflected in the fact that 19 (38%) have been awarded Grade 1 status on the national Statutory Register of Listed Buildings. For comparison, in the considerably larger neighbouring county of Leicestershire, there are just 64 Grade 1 churches (somewhat less than 20%). In Simon Jenkins much quoted 'England's 1000 Best Churches' book he selects 13 Rutland churches for inclusion (slightly more than 25% of the total number in the county), while only 16 (around 5% of the total number) are chosen from Leicestershire. These figures tell the story of the popularity Rutland's churches enjoy, and it is no surprise that they appear in many books about the nation's churches, often in proportionally larger numbers than other larger counties. Churches such as Exton, Ketton, Stoke Dry, Tickencote and Tixover are almost fixtures in generalist churches books. However, there are few books that deal solely with Rutland churches. Spiegl Press of Stamford specialise in books about Rutland and several of their books refer to the county's churches in passing, but two titles are concerned solely with them. These are 'Churches of Rutland' (Prophet & Traylen, 1988) and the recent 'The Parish Churches of Rutland' (Collett, 2012). Cantor (2000) describes 19 Rutland churches in detail and refers to some others elsewhere in the text. And of course Pevsner (2003) is as indispensable for Rutland churches and other buildings as he is for everywhere else in the country. That great champion of the East Midlands, W. G. Hoskins, first published his 'Rutland A Shell Guide' in 1949 and it remains a very readable, if necessarily constrained, account of the settlements and their churches. Mee (1st edn, 1937) comes under the same heading, but is more anecdotal and subjective. In the early 2000's Rutland County Council produced a very useful (and free) open-out pamphlet which describes highlights of 15 Rutland churches; this is also available for download online. Brandwood (2002) contains brief notes on the C19th restoration of Rutland's churches. For books that deal with the architecture, archaeology and fittings of churches, there are several excellent recent publications e.g. Taylor (2003), Fewins (2005) and McNamara and Tilney (2011). However, for sheer readability and depth of information, it is still difficult to better 'The Observer's Book of old English Churches' (Jones, 1965), and almost anything on churches by Sir John Betjeman is well worth reading. Many churches produce their own guides to their buildings, which vary from glossy colour mini-books to a single A4 sheet. These can be excellent sources of information, sometimes with extra local detail missing from the literature elsewhere, but their availability can be erratic.

The internet was of great assistance and these days is indispensable to any researcher. As a resource of information it has proved to be nothing less than revolutionary. Having The Victoria History of the County of Rutland (volume II, 1935) freely available online (http://www.british-history.ac.uk/source.aspx?pubid=528) has been a terrific boon, and the sections on the churches of each settlement have been constant reference points. Almost equally useful was the British Listed Buildings website at http://www.britishlistedbuildings.co.uk/, which lists and describes all the buildings on the national Statutory Register of Listed Buildings. These two sites were core resources for information on Rutland's churches, but other sites contributed supplemental details, including http://www.rutlandchurches.co.uk/, http://greatenglishchurches.co.uk/html/rutland.html and http://english-church-architecture.net/. Also, some churches publish historical and architectural details of their buildings on their websites, and some of these are very informative.

Books

Brandwood, G. K. 2002. Bringing them to their knees: church building and restoration in Leicestershire and Rutland 1800-1914. Leicestershire Archaeological and Historical Society, Leicester.

Collett, P. 2012. The Parish Churches of Rutland. Spiegl Press, Stamford.

Cantor, L. 2000. The Historic Parish Churches of Leicestershire and Rutland. Kairos Press, Newtown Linford, Leicester.

Fewins, C. 2005. The church explorers handbook. Canterbury Press, Norwich.

Harvey, A. and Crowther-Beynon, V. B. 1912. Leicestershire and Rutland. Little Guides series. Methuen & Co. Ltd., London.

Hoskins, W. G. 1949. Rutland: a Shell Guide. Faber & Faber, London.

Jenkins, S. 2009. England's thousand best churches. Penguin Books.

Jones, L. E. 1965. The Observer's book of old English churches. Warne, London.

McNamara, D. R. and Tilney, H. 2011. How to read churches: a crash course in ecclesiastical architecture. A. and C. Black (Publishers), London.

Mee, A. 1937. The King's England. Leicestershire and Rutland. Hodder & Stoughton, London.

Pevsner, N. 2003. The Buildings of England. Leicestershire and Rutland. Revised by Williamson, E. Yale University Press, New Haven.

Prophet. J. and Traylen, A. R. 1988. Churches of Rutland. Volume 11 'In Rutland' series. Spiegl Press, Stamford.

Taylor, R. 2003. How to read a church: a guide to images, symbols and meanings in churches and cathedrals. Rider, London.

Trubshaw, B. 2004. Good Gargoyle Guide. Medieval carvings in Leicestershire and Rutland. Heart of Albion Press, Wymeswold, Loughborough.

Whitelaw, J. W. 1996. Hidden Leicestershire and Rutland. Countryside Books, Newbury.

Websites

http://english-church-architecture.net/

http://greatenglishchurches.co.uk/html/rutland.html

http://www.discover-rutland.co.uk/xsdbimgs/PDF's/RutlandChurchTrailLeaflet.pdf

http://www.british-history.ac.uk/source.aspx?pubid=528

http://www.britishlistedbuildings.co.uk/england/rutland

http://www.rutlandchurches.co.uk/

Church Guides/leaflets

Anon. 1996. St Peter Brooke. A history & guide.

_____ 2011. Holy Trinity Teigh

_____ 2013. The parish church of St Mary the Virgin Ketton. Church Guide.

Anon. n.d. St Mary's Ashwell, Rutland.

_____ n.d. A brief guide to the parish church of St Peter Belton in Rutland

_____ n.d. Parish church of St John the Evangelist (Caldecott).

____ n.d. St Nicholas Cottesmore.

____ n.d. St Edmund King & Martyr Egleton.

____ n.d. Empingham, Rutland. Church and village.

____ n.d. St Peter & St Paul church Great Casterton.

____ n.d. St Mary the Virgin parish church Greetham. Church Guide.

____ n.d. Saint Andrew's Church Hambleton.

____ n.d. St Peter and St Paul Langham.

____ n.d. All Saints Church Little Casterton.

____ n.d. Welcome to St Nicholas Church Pilton.

____ n.d. A brief history of Seaton All Hallows church.

____ n.d. St Mary the Virgin South Luffenham Rutland. Church Guide.

____ n.d. St Andrew, Stoke Dry.

____ n.d. A short guide to the church of St Peter, Tickencote.

____ n.d. A brief guide to All Saints church Tinwell.

____ n.d. The history of St Luke's church Tixover.

____ n.d. Church of Saint Botolph, Wardley.

____ n.d. Church Guide. Welcome to St Andrew's church Whissendine.

Aston, N. 2003. All Saints Oakham. A guide and history.

Bisseker, R. G. & Irons, E. A. 2010. The parish church of St Michael & All Angels Whitwell Rutland.

Coldwell, W. S. G. 1985. Notes on St Peter's church, Tickencote.

Moubray, J. & M. 2010. The church of St Mary Magdalene & St Andrew Ridlington.

Tew, D. 1971. A history of the parish and church of Wing Rutland.

Waites, B., Sleath, S. & Ovens, R. 1984. Normanton Church Rutland Water.

A last word – the top ten

I consider the following to be the 10 churches in Rutland that should be visited above all others, although I must point out that this doesn't mean they are the *best* or the ones that anyone else would choose, this is purely a personal view and in random order.

Stoke Dry, Langham, Ketton, Tixover, Tickencote, Brooke, Exton, Morcott, Whissendine and Ryhall.

Visit all the others as well, don't forget to leave a donation and sign the visitor's book!

Andrew Swift, June 2014

Brooke St Peter